Working Choices

Working Choices

New Perspectives on Work and Career

Bob Mendonsa

Writers Club Press

San Jose New York Lincoln Shanghai

Working Choices
New Perspectives on Work and Career

Writers Club Press
an imprint of iUniverse.com, Inc.

For information address:
iUniverse.com, Inc.
620 North 48th Street, Suite 201
Lincoln, NE 68504-3467
www.iuniverse.com

ISBN: 0-595-12238-8

Printed in the United States of America

This book is dedicated to my sons, Jeremy and Timothy Mendonsa, and to the wonderful people I have worked with over the years.

CONTENTS

Acknowledgements ix

Introduction xi

Part One: The Experience of Working
          inside an Organization 1

    Caution Label *3*

    Really, It's Not All Bad *5*

    The Rules of the Status Game *26*

    The Corporate Control Fetish *47*

    Everything but the Truth *66*

    The Curious Notion of Leadership *86*

    To Choose or Not to Choose *101*

Part Two: Creating Responsible Choices 117

    A New Perspective on Responsibility *119*

    Self-Responsibility *140*

    Responsibility to Others *170*

Responsibility to Community *188*

Responsibility in the Workplace *203*

About the Author 219

Appendix: Working Arenas...221

References 243

ACKNOWLEDGEMENTS

I wish to thank Terri Robberson for her careful editing and listening skills, to say nothing of her emotional and spiritual support during the writing process.

Introduction

There are always choices. I could have taken the Redwood Highway and treated myself to a leisurely drive near the fog-cooled California coast. The presence of two young boys, aged thirteen and ten, made that option less than appealing. They had no interest in scenery, no matter how sublime. Like good high-tech children everywhere, they valued high speed. So instead of communing with the gentle giants of the forest and experiencing the grandeur of waves crashing against the cliffs, I found myself whizzing up I–5 through the dry flatlands of the Northern Central Valley. Instead of opening my windows to the cool ocean breeze, we shut them tight against the one hundred-degree heat as we sped through a galaxy of alfalfa fields interrupted every thirty miles by rest stops bulging with Winnebagos and coffee shops drenched in beige vinyl.

My sons and I were on our way to Oregon for a week's vacation. Even with the speed of the interstate, we were numb by the time we hit Red Bluff. We had played the alphabet game, listened to every cassette and covered all the plans for the trip at least twice. The only option I could come up with was conversation. The less-than-inspiring environment outside the car windows led me to ask a less-than-inspiring question.

"So, what do you guys want to be when you grow up?"

The youngest didn't know. He liked music and basketball and Star Trek, but he hadn't yet translated any of those interests into a promising career direction by his eleventh year on the planet.

My eldest, however, expressed no doubt whatsoever on this subject.

"A software engineer," he replied without skipping a beat. "That way I could design all sorts of cool software and I wouldn't have to wear a freaking tie to work."

My immediate reaction was an anxiety attack bordering on panic. Although I had chosen to spend most of my adult life in various work settings and though I was now earning my daily bread trying to improve life in different organizations, I reacted with a combination of shock, dismay and overbearing parentalism.

"Why in the hell do you want a goddamn job?" I shouted at him.

I was paying too much attention to the road to take in his reaction but his silence revealed a mixture of shock and confusion. He was probably sitting there wondering, "Isn't getting a job what you're supposed to do?" and thinking that his father was getting crotchety in his old age. I found myself wondering about my sanity as well, because I wasn't really sure why I had reacted with such emotional velocity to the possibility that my son would have a job some day. Shoving a cassette into the player and cranking up the volume, I retreated into my thoughts to search for an answer.

Something inside me had rebelled at the thought of my children following the path of millions of other upstanding citizens and entering the workforce. The vision of my offspring spending all day in one boring meeting after another or stuck on the shop floor with repetitive, tedious work was appalling. I couldn't imagine these creative, spontaneous human beings having to go through the pain and drudgery of an existence marked by power trips, status games and senseless bureaucratic territoriality. The thought of these naturally open and honest little people becoming confused and helpless as they experienced the vacuum of truth that pervades many organizations made my stomach turn.

"Oh, Jesus, not a job! Anything but a goddamn job!" I screamed out of the blue after about ten minutes of silence. Out of the corner of my eye I saw my sons exchange meaningful looks. *He's totally losing it.*

I took the traditional parental emergency exit. "I'll explain it later," I said.

The Default Choice

The dominant pattern of modern life has not changed much in the last fifty years: go-to-school-get-a-job-get-married-settle-down-raise-a-family-get-a-watch-retire. If you are one of the unfortunate souls who were not born into streams of inherited wealth, you have probably followed all or part of this pattern, depending on how far you've advanced in the aging process.

However, it is clear that the pattern is unraveling. Marriage is not the sacred institution it once was, and if you're not heterosexual, it is not an option in most places. Having children is no longer an automatic choice for growing numbers of women; I once worked in a department with nine other women, all but one over thirty, all but one childless and the rest with no plans or even thoughts of either getting married or raising kids. The get-a-watch concept is fading fast, as corporations switch their propaganda from "job security" to "job opportunity," meaning that any loyalty you have to a company had better be of the flexible variety. Retirement itself is undergoing flux, as rich yuppies try to accelerate their savings to either retire early or to ensure that they'll have something to spend during their golden years, since they are unconvinced that Social Security will survive that long.

But the go-to-school-get-a-job part of the pattern is still holding firm. There are a few artistic types who manage to avoid it, and few entrepreneurs who have parlayed their talents and marketing savvy into relative independence, but for most of us slobs, the menu is pretty much limited to a list of possible occupations. Some opt out of going to college and have to select from a shorter menu. Those who go to college begin with more choices, but those choices are eventually reduced by the push to specialize in a single body of knowledge. People see jobs as a necessary evil, a sign that you have matured and are willing to accept reality for what it is—a daily routine of commute, work and commute again. They are things we "have to get," not necessarily things we "want to get."

That last statement would appear to contradict recent Gallup Poll results that show that 86% of Americans are satisfied with their jobs. However, since the same poll also indicates that about two-thirds of the populace would either leave or change their jobs if they hit the lottery, one can argue quite persuasively that most people are not at all satisfied with their employment. My experience tells me that people often like what they do but they despise their leaders or the general working environment. But there is more to it than that, something elusive that cannot be captured in polling numbers.

Having listened to thousands of people in all kinds of organizations for a period of over twenty years, I can say unequivocally that tune I hear most often in the background is Peggy Lee singing "Is That All There Is?" This does not show up in polls on job satisfaction because people have a hard time telling the truth about their current status. We always say things are going better than they are because we don't want anyone to think we've made a mistake. This applies to everything from buying a new car (it's always "I love this car" even if it is a lemon) to choosing a job. Since people learn to put on a happy face for their employers to avoid being labeled complainers or to prevent having their career paths filled with landmines planted by resentful bosses, any survey of the workplace is but a superficial indication of what is really going on. The reality is more along the lines of the common response, "It's okay—for a job."

The employment scene is like a bad supermarket. There are plenty of items to choose from, but none of them really satisfy the craving. Many of the items are attractively packaged, but when we open the packaging, the contents are either flat or spoiled. We stand in the aisles like Mary Tyler Moore during the opening credits trying to decide if we really want the thing in our hands and then shrug our shoulders and fling it into the cart. After all, we have to eat something.

Among the selections available to us, the default choice for most people is some kind of job in a corporation. Government isn't doing much hiring these days (unless you really want to be a horribly underpaid customs-and-immigration officer), and since the new generation enter-ing the workforce does not seem to possess the same level of idealism that their hippie parents eventually abandoned, non-profits are not seen as a serious option. This leaves us with the business world, particularly if your overriding "need" is to make money. Landing a prestigious job at an up-and-coming corporation (preferably a dot.com) that offers stock options to its new hires is considered a high-class move, representing the latest model of the American dream. However, those positions are few and far between. The bottom line is we go to work for corporations because corporations have the jobs, and competitively speaking, they do a much better job of attracting candidates than the government (who will be happy to send you a five-pound application packet) or most non-profits (who rarely get around to advertising because there's too much work to be done).

Unfortunately, once you get past the corporate packaging that adver-tises a constantly expanding career path and the apparently attractive job offer, you have to go to work at the place. The reality of the workplace is very different from what most people expect. Prospective employers don't tell you that it is impossible to get anything done in their corporation because of a power struggle on the executive level. Recruiters don't tell you that your boss is an arrogant jerk who always has to be right and that if you have the gall to suggest new ways of doing things, they will banish you to an outer cubicle to clean up an ancient database. Sometimes an old hand will see your excited face as you enter the workplace with your sugar plum visions, pull you aside and whisper, "Wait until you've been here about six months." That's usually how long it takes for people to realize that their chances of making a real difference in an organization are virtually nil.

This is not to imply that all corporations are this way and that everyone working in a corporation is a self-serving, self-righteous incompetent. If that were the case, corporations would not have produced the successes they have produced. Most organizations survive and sometimes thrive because of a small core of decent, dedicated human beings with a strong orientation towards cooperation who somehow work through all the crap strewn in their paths like Andy Dufresne crawling through the sewer to freedom in *The Shawshank Redemption*. These people are both fortunate and determined enough to find both meaning and achievement in their work. Though some are in positions of leadership, most tend to work quietly in the background, translating the gibberish emanating from above or from "corporate" into workable solutions that satisfy customers and earn profits for the enterprise. They are people who can turn lemons into lemonade, living proof that spending one's life in an organization can be a rewarding, personally satisfying experience.

So while it is possible to retire with more than a gold watch but also with one's dignity, there is more than enough pain in any organization to make job satisfaction a very difficult thing to achieve. One could read the Gallup Poll and feel reassured that America is a happy place full of happy workers who cannot wait for Monday morning. If that were true, why are stress management classes in such great demand? The survey results do not capture the overwhelming dissatisfaction with the greater predicament of an employment system that seems to offer us a limited set of less-than-desirable options. The poll only measures what we have learned to cope with, learned to accept as normal and our ability to give up when faced with what we perceive to be the inevitable. The poll fails to capture what is really going on.

What's really going on is that our organizations are filled with people who don't really want to be there and would much rather be doing something else.

Victims of the System

I learned all this through years of commiserating with co-workers on coffee breaks and later through years of listening to the problems of the inhabitants of corporations in my human resources and organizational change jobs. While I was trained to be a good active listener and to be humanistic in the extreme, I also have to admit there were times when I'd had more than my fill of sour grapes. At those moments, I would usually explode with, "Then why the hell don't you go somewhere else?"

The answers I got were very revealing. All doubted that they could get something elsewhere that was as good as what they had. None wanted to let go of the investment they had made in time, energy and "belief in the cause." Primarily, they did not want to believe that their contribution was of no consequence or meaning, especially after all the years of toil they had poured into the place.

And every one of them cited financial or other obligations in the end. "I can't leave—I have a mortgage and mouths to feed." "Oh, yeah, if I hit Lotto tomorrow, I'm out of here." I realized that these were extremely effective people trapped by a choice made long ago: to work for an organization in the first place. To decide to get a goddamn job.

That is the question that we will explore in this book: do you really want to spend a good part of your future inside an organization? Do you really want a job? If not, what are your options? These are questions we cannot take lightly, for work takes up a good portion of our lives and an even greater portion of our available energies. For too long, we have acted as if that choice was already made for us and that our responsibility was to simply pick from whatever jobs were available. What this book demonstrates is that any time we accept a default choice, any time we make a decision without full awareness of the consequences, we cannot live up to three core responsibilities: the responsibility we have to ourselves, the responsibility we have to others and the responsibility we have to our communities. We become victims of the system or mere drones instead of thinking, active, responsible adults. When that happens, everyone suffers: the people we work with, the organization, and most painfully, ourselves.

People who currently have jobs can use the book and the exercises to reflect on their current situation and develop a future direction. Students considering their options can apply the material to various options before making life plans. After all, no one is condemned to spend the rest of their lives following the same routine. "Why get up and repeat yesterday's song-and-dance?" asked Henry Miller, who then packed in his job as a corporate recruiter for a typewriter in Paris. Whatever your current circumstances, this book can help you make intelligent choices about an activity that contributes enormously to your happiness or unhappiness: your work.

This book focuses more on the arenas of employment (the larger environments like corporations, government, non-profits, etc.) than occupations. If you feel your primary need is to select an occupation, there are innumerable career development books and services available to you. However, the problems people face at work have little to do with the job itself and a whole lot more to do with the working environment. The common complaint is "I'd wish they'd leave me alone so I can get some work done." Even if you are perfectly suited for a particular job, that does not translate into job satisfaction unless you are also compatible with the arena in which you work. That aspect of the choice is often ignored because the evils of organizations and corporations in particular are often taken as an inevitable part of the bargain. Any time a person skirts over an aspect of a particular choice without considering the consequences, the final decision invariably turns out a disappointment.

Here we will examine the larger arenas, with particular emphasis on the default choice of the corporation. Because there are many similarities between corporations and other kinds of organizations when it comes to dynamics such as status, control and truth-avoidance, we have simplified the tale by focusing on the generic corporation. In one sense, what we are doing in this book is talking about the "ropes" you are supposed to learn through experience once you enter the workplace. By reflecting on some of the underlying assumptions of organizational life, the goal is to give you more accurate information about what it is really like to work inside an organization. This is in keeping with a fundamental tenet of the book, that the quality of choices is always improved by learning, which in turn is facilitated by access to information. The overriding purpose of this book is to help prevent the tendency to make unconscious choices about our working lives so we can experience more satisfaction in our work.

Reflections on Responsibility

One theme we will repeat ad infinitum is that we cannot understand organizations apart from the society in which they exist. Most of the significant problems in organizations have nothing to do with skill-building or systems analysis or even a lack of understanding of the competitive marketplace. The chronic problems that exist in organizations are merely reflections of crises in the larger culture. If we have violence in our society, it will follow that we will have violence in our workplaces. If the culture is in flux regarding sexual roles, it makes perfect sense that our organizations would be equally neurotic about gender issues.

The cultural norms that wreak havoc in the workplace involve status, control, truth, leadership and our convoluted definitions of responsibility. These are all issues about which Americans are either completely confused or completely divided. We proclaim our belief in equality while playing petty status games with each other and transferring the competitiveness of the marketplace to our dealings inside the workplace. We get misty-eyed when reminded of our cherished belief in freedom on the Fourth of July and then do everything we can to stop people from exercising freedom of thought or action in the course of their jobs. For all of our prattling about truth, we fail to find it in our media, in our leaders, in our courtrooms or even in our own conversations on any consistent, reliable basis. We exalt our leaders and vilify them in the same breath; Bill Gates is currently both the most admired and most hated person in America.

All of these issues intersect at one point: the issue of responsibility. We will explore that in great detail in the second half of the book, but for a snapshot view of the crisis, I offer the following observation of American society taken from the British author Ben Elton and his book *Popcorn*:

"Nothing is anybody's fault. We don't do wrong, we have problems. We're victims, alcoholics, sexaholics. Do you know you can be a shopaholic? That's right. People aren't greedy anymore, oh no. They're shopaholics, victims of commercialism. Victims! People don't fail any more. They experience negative success. We are building a culture of gutless, spineless, self-righteous whining cry-babies who have an excuse for everything and take responsibility for nothing."

We can add to Elton's observations that as a people starving for any indication of responsibility, and as a people terrified of admitting human weakness or simple human error, we engage in the sport of blaming with great passion and energy. Our avoidance of accepting fault is directly attributable to the defense mechanisms that have become part of our collective personality as the result of years of finger-pointing and hunting for scapegoats. Organizations are places where we have chosen blame as the preferred tactic for dealing with any unpleasantness that comes our way.

Whether or not we are a greedy, neurotic, violent, paranoid, thrill-seeking people interested only in money, flash and instant gratification (as Elton describes us in Popcorn) is a debate that we will not carry forward in this book. We are interested in how our cultural traits, both negative and positive, play out in the course of our daily work. For trying to understand an organization without considering the larger culture is like trying to figure out the behavior of a planet without considering the gravitational pull of its star. Our organizations are both by-products of our culture and contributors to our culture, and we will not solve the problems in either realm until we address the problems that connect both.

Structure

Another fundamental premise of this book is that both individuals and organizations would be much better off if people would consider their choices about work with more care and forethought than they do at present. Most people stumble into their jobs through a chain of circumstances that rarely includes conscious thought. "I was just going to work here for a year until I could save for college," one thirty-year employee of a Fortune 500 company told me. As I describe in a later chapter, I have rarely met an individual in a corporation who is doing what he or she really wants to be doing. This should be an astonishing revelation, but most people simply accept the fact that they're stuck.

This book is about showing people that they're not at all stuck, that in fact they do have choices. The first part of the book takes us through the positives and negatives of making the default choice of corporate employment by describing what it's really like to work in most corporations. Self-reflection exercises appear in each chapter so the reader can evaluate his or her own experiences in organizations. The second section considers the possibility of living a life in a more conscious, responsible manner, which may lead to a job in a corporation, but then again, may not. In the process, we redefine responsibility to cleanse the word of any connotation of blame or guilt and use that new definition as the basis of several self-help exercises designed to assist the reader in creating alternative futures more in line with their desires and abilities. The final chapter is for those of you who decide to stay in corporate life and wish to go about changing it.

The goal is that by the end of the book, you will either know why the hell you want a job or why the hell you don't.

Sources

This book draws on my experience in listening to thousands of people in organizations over the years. Having worked in employee relations, human resources and organizational development, much of my experience has revolved around the difficulties people face in the workplace. Over the years, I have heard many stories from all kinds of people at all organizational levels, from the manufacturing floor to the professional cubicles to the executive suite. Some of the stories were unintentionally humorous, like the one about the employee who was unable to work effectively because she was brooding about having sent her husband to the hospital after a round of vigorous lovemaking. Some were tragic, like hearing a person I'd known for several years tell me he was HIV-positive. Some were chilling, as when a supervisor and I sat down to listen to an employee tell us how he intended to murder one of his co-workers. For the most part, though, the stories were of people searching for meaning. The storytellers were, for the most part, decent and well-meaning people who were frustrated about the way things were going on the job and having a hard time understanding why things had to be the way they were. They wanted things to be different but didn't know how to go about making things different. They were also struggling with themselves, with who they were and what they were doing. Often they would question their own abilities and come down hard on themselves in the search for answers.

They are the people to whom this book is dedicated, the people who go into an organization with the best intentions, who persevere in the face of near-insanity and try to make a difference. I listened to their stories under a promise of confidentiality, and I will continue to respect that here. I will also protect the confidentiality of the organizations involved and not mention the names of any companies in this book. I choose to do this for two reasons. First, I do not intend to feed the general human appetite for scapegoats, and corporations are cheap and easy targets for people looking for something to blame. Second, many authors on the subject of organizational life have made the mistake of citing companies for excellence only to see the company go down in flames a year or two later. By classifying specific organizations positively or negatively, I would run the risk of making the book obsolete. Organizations can change, and bad companies can become good ones, and vice versa.

But first, let's take a look at what they're really like.

Part One:

The Experience of Working inside an Organization

CAUTION LABEL

Important: Read This Before Proceeding!
Author Does Not Assume Liability for the
Consequences of Skipping This Little Chapter

One of the early stages in organizational change work involves surfacing the problems the organization faces. This is not simply a matter of listening to the executives tell you what they think the problems are. Most of the problems that plague organizations are things that people do not openly discuss, at least in polite company. Over the years people become conditioned to taking the organization as it is, partially because they have no hope of changing it. Surfacing the real problems accomplishes two things. One, it enables the organization to face its true challenges instead of chasing symptoms and ghosts. Second, it allows people to release all the pent-up anger and frustration so they can move off it and onto more productive tasks.

The danger is, of course, that some people don't want to move off it. They want to identify who is responsible for the mess they find themselves in and invariably they identify the organization's leaders as the guilty parties.

"Au contraire," I always tell them. "Organizations are human creations and we have all played a part in what has happened here. None of us are victims of an impersonal system or of leaders who spend all night figuring out ways to exploit us. You want to know who created this mess? Look in the mirror! We did it! We did it all by ourselves!"

People usually resist this wisdom because they don't want to accept responsibility for the choice they made years ago to join the organization in the first place. We usually create a psychological "out" by telling ourselves we're really repressed artists or that we really belong on the golf circuit and that "someday" it will come. This gives us a justification for disassociating ourselves from the organization's problems.

This is an unfortunate misperception that serves no one. When we join an organization, we unwittingly but willingly submit to the ways of the organization, accepting and validating those ways by our mere presence. We cannot separate ourselves from what is happening, for that would be a basic denial of reality. We are there. Our presence activates a sense of responsibility to the community of the workplace, and though we may go through hoops to try to deny its existence, that sense of responsibility is always present, even if we only experience it as that little twinge of guilt we feel when we're not doing our best. I point this out now because as you read through the following chapters, you will no doubt look for someone to hold up for judgment. Some of the realities of corporate life are appalling and when we are appalled, we want to hunt down the guilty and bring them to justice. Therefore, please take note of the following and return to this page whenever you feel the urge to take it out on the idiots surrounding you in the workplace:

> *Organizations are above all human creations. We create and sustain them for our own personal reasons. If you want to know who is responsible for the state of any given organization, don't look up, look in the mirror.*

Before we catalog the crimes, let's review the good news. Believe it or not, there are good things about working in a corporation.

REALLY, IT'S NOT ALL BAD

No matter how much we hate getting up on Monday morning and no matter how much we complain about our organizations, we obviously consider jobs valuable commodities. Why else would millions of people spend enormous quantities of time and energy trying to secure something if that something had no value? Why would we insist that our youth structure their lives around doing what they need to do to realize success in the job market if jobs were not a fundamentally enriching experience? Surely we would not wish to condemn our children to lifetimes lacking value and meaning. We must assume, therefore, that there are good things about having a job and will use this chapter to identify what those things are.

Paying Up

The refrain you usually hear when you ask unhappy people why they are working is the line, "It pays the bills." This response implies that "the bills" are unavoidable burdens. It further suggests that we are chained to our jobs because we have no choice but to meet our financial obligations.

It is true that a regular job provides a consistent source of money. The consistency of this income varies with the compensation plan, but generally speaking, reliable employment translates into reliable income. This regularity gives people certain advantages by allowing them to plan for the future. Thus we can buy houses for our families and occasionally spring for a new car. Self-employed individuals are at a disadvantage in this regard, because their income is not as predictable. Therefore, one of the advantages of having a job is indeed the fact that "it pays the bills," because it gives us confidence that the money will be there to meet current obligations and incur new ones.

However, there are several things about this justification that do not ring true. If we are honest with ourselves, we have to admit that most bills beyond food, basic clothing, basic shelter and other necessities are the result of personal preference or individual greed. For most people, having the secure income of a steady job only leads to more spending and more bills. Despite the evidence of frequent and often massive layoffs in the corporate sector, the regularity of that paycheck lulls us into the belief that it will always be there, leading us to create new obligations with too much ease for our own good. Bills are indeed burdens but they are burdens we choose to carry.

We also know that having a job is in itself expensive, because having one creates new expenses that we didn't have before. Beyond commute and clothing expenses, there are dozens of hidden costs in having a job. These include: contributing to a co-worker's birthday gift; laying out a couple of bucks on the football pool; being shamed by the company into contributing to their favorite charity; or feeling like you have to buy a couple of those peculiar chocolate bars that working parents of high schoolers foist on their colleagues every school year. Taking into account the remarkable talent of most Americans to spend far beyond their means, it is safe to say that we waste a good two-thirds of our take-home pay on stuff we didn't really want or need in the first place or on the trappings of employment itself.

People who have jobs and tell you that they work to pay the bills will also tell you, "It's important to get ahead." What they mean by this is that it is important to continue to seek higher status and more money, because then, according to the myth, you will have more choices. Anyone who has moved up the ladders of a corporation will tell you that this is not always the case. People usually use the extra money to buy more expensive versions of the same thing, be it cars, stereos or houses. We rarely if ever get ahead to the point where we do not feel we need a job to pay the bills. While more money translates to more options in a free market society like ours, we have to point out that increasing the quantity of choice does not increase the quality of choice. Getting ahead and making more money may mean more choices, but we do not really apply ourselves very well to making the choices that we dream about making, like taking a year off to stay at home with the kids or sail around the world. A few months after the big promotion, we feel just as trapped as we did before opportunity came our way.

While many people have told me that they work primarily for the money, the desire for money does not necessarily translate into having to have a job. There are hundreds of other ways to earn a living, many of which may be far more appealing than having to live your life by the clock and put up with the insanity of the daily commute. No, there must be other considerations at work here, considerations that allow us to put up with the sometimes painful, sometimes laughable but always demanding life inside an organization.

Let's take a look at those other considerations.

Continuity and Stability

Having a job means more continuity and stability in one's life. Going to work every day helps order our existence, and human beings like a sense of order in their lives. While well-publicized layoffs and reorganizations have compromised the traditional meaning of security, having a job is a more ordered reality than working in the arts or starting your own business. The regularity of the weekly schedule provides a relatively stable structure for our lives.

This is no small advantage for those who prefer routine and relative calm. Although organizations can go crazy, every organization provides a routine even if it is simply the routine of going to the same workstation every day or attending those dreadful weekly meetings. With the pace of change speeding up in every aspect of life, these little routines can help keep a person grounded. Of course, workplaces are changing with as much velocity as the rest of society, but when change appears in a familiar context, it's a little easier to take. After all, even when management is busy implementing change after change, you still have your co-workers to rely on for a good gripe session. Even when reorganizations wipe out half of those co-workers, there is still the rhythm of going to the same place at the same time every day (assuming you survive the reorganization).

Our love of order is a two-edged sword, as our need for predictability can interfere with our ability to perceive new opportunities and consider new ideas. We get very stubborn when someone is messing with our personal sense of order. However, when the need to preserve routine becomes more important than the universal need to learn and grow, we stagnate. Because organizations reinforce our natural preference for order with endless rules and regulations, life in an organization can become so regimented that we start working far below our capabilities. With these serious dangers in mind, however, we can say that organizations do provide relative (underline relative) stability in a world characterized by rapid technological and social change. If routine is for you, consider the standard model job and forget free-lance photography or modern dance.

Self-Worth

Organizations give people the opportunity to work, which may sound painfully obvious, but is nevertheless an important consideration. Many people who have tried to go out on their own simply do not know what to do with their time. Organizations usually have jobs that can not only pass the time but also give a person a chance to exercise hidden talents or even artistry by providing a structure for one's efforts.

People naturally seek competence and many people have found competence by working in organizations. That they often have to realize this competence against the best efforts of the organization to screw things up for them makes it even more of a challenge and hence increases the psychological payoff.

I remember sitting down for a whole day with a collector who demonstrated this truism. The job of a bill collector is a pretty crummy job. You have to call people who would prefer you did not exist and demand that they meet their obligations. People who are behind in their payments are often rude, defensive and obnoxious. In addition to the traditional hazards associated with collections, the company had given her no training on the computer system, a system that could only be classified as a nightmare, consisting of three separate systems that did not communicate with each other. Despite the obstacles, I watched with increasing admiration as she calmly analyzed each call, changed roles with the ease of Laurence Olivier to suit the kind of personality on the other end of the phone, and through a complex system of Post-Its and outdated reports, managed to outwit the computer system that was trying so hard to frustrate her efforts. By the end of the day, she had creamed her goals and went home ready to spend the night partying, in a good mood from having beat both the odds and the system.

The fact that organizations are often screwed up gives people a chance to do work they never thought they were capable of doing. When there is no one else around to do an important job, someone has to step in and do it. In these situations, a person can learn new skills and find themselves the recipient of genuine appreciation from a panicked manager who didn't have a clue about what to do. The myth of the career ladder where working life is a predictable climb in a single field is a fast-dissolving myth, disappearing in the face of a new market reality that demands daily flexibility. Organizations, therefore, give the average person a chance to do new stuff, which is always a good thing, no matter how much that individual might prefer routine. As such, working for a living can build self-worth by giving people the opportunity to stretch themselves.

Of course, the opposite is also true. Working in many organizations can destroy a person's self-confidence, particularly if they are unlucky enough to draw a manipulative or abusive manager. Still, the human drive for meaning is very powerful and I have frequently seen people develop confidence as the result of overcoming numerous obstacles, including hopeless leaders.

Community

Having a job means belonging to an organization, which for many people living in the twenty-first century is as close to being a part of a community as they're going to get.

There are very few opportunities for working people to become involved in their society, because they simply do not have the time. Besides the sheer number of hours we spend on the job, we also spend a great deal of time getting ready for work, commuting to the workplace and coming home again at night. Who has time for the PTA, Little League, the Human Rights Campaign or the city council meeting? People want time to unwind, relax, eat dinner, party, have sex, watch their favorite television shows, exercise, surf the Web, build a treehouse, help their kids with their homework…and becoming involved in the neighborhood or local politics is a low priority task.

This loss of local community may be more acute in heavily urbanized areas due to the time involved in commuting, but there are other influences at work here. The corporate cost-cutting moves that began in the 1980's required people to put in more hours, largely because the efficiencies that re-engineering and new technology promised were often no more than wishful thinking. It now seems odd to watch movies from the early age of computers (like *The Desk Set* with Spencer Tracy and Katharine Hepburn) and realize that people were afraid of losing their jobs to computers. While this sometimes happens today, it is just as plausible to argue that computers and other new technologies have created more work for people because of the inherent problems and possibilities associated with having them. One thing is certain, though: the life of the average person revolves around the workplace—not the church, not the town hall, and not the neighborhood drinking hole. Our work has become our lives.

Therefore, organizations play an important role in society by providing some form of community and regular human interaction to the average person who may not get it otherwise. The workplace is where we celebrate birthdays and new babies, where we commiserate about divorces and deaths in the families, where we watch each other develop and mature. Along with marriages, workplaces provide us with those dwindling opportunities for getting pissed off at someone and making up later. We make friends in the workplace and often find that our social circle consists largely of co-workers. Often we meet our mates in the workplace, despite the best efforts of legal and personnel professionals to stamp out romance in organizations.

Oddly enough, though, many workers do not appreciate the social interaction provided by the workplace and many of the people I know would much rather work at home. Part of this has to do with the avoidance of commute, of dress codes and of office politics; much of it has to do with the fact that the home sometimes offers a better venue for actually getting one's work done. Some people like it because it allows them to remain closer to their children. If we all become telecommuters, though, we will need to come up with something to replace the loss of community, for chatting on the Internet is no substitute for face-to-face contact. The camaraderie one can build with a group of co-workers is one of the best arguments for pursuing a regular job. Although most workgroups in organizations are incredibly dysfunctional due to poor facilitation and the energy drain created by purposeless staff meetings, groups can sometimes accomplish miracles, and there is nothing quite as special as the feeling of shared success resulting from shared effort.

Organizations, then, give people the opportunity to contribute to something larger than themselves, an important outlet for any healthy human being. That so few organizations encourage this should not discount the possibility of meaningful contribution to a community. It is an opportunity rarely afforded the consultant or the independent contractor, who are never there long enough to appreciate their impact on community life. Some organizations enhance the feeling of community by recognizing their responsibility to society, forming groups of volunteer employees who contribute time or money to neighborhoods or charitable groups. This is particularly helpful when the company itself is making something that is completely useful but also completely meaningless, like screws or postage meters.

Fascinating People

The community of an organization consists of people with varied backgrounds and life experiences. There are people with unusual histories and people who have done the go-to-school-get-a-job-raise-a-family trip. In the better organizations, there are people from different cultures, but even in poorly run organizations there is always a degree of diversity operating in the sense that each individual has a slightly different twist on life. The journeys people have taken to arrive at a particular organization often make for interesting stories, as there are very few people in an organization anywhere who are doing what they wanted to do before they grew up. Through my work in corporations, I have met poets, musicians and artists; heard tales from soldiers, sailors and mercenaries; rubbed shoulders with inventors, philosophers and even a few psychics.

But the best part is that there are some people working in organizations who really do make a difference.

There is a core group in any organization who keep the place going with their tireless efforts and superhuman responsiveness to the needs of the organization's clients and customers. They survive through good and lean years, through competent and incompetent leaders, through significant change and insignificant stability. They always seem to be willing to help, always volunteering for the next assignment and always engaged in the enterprise with their hearts and souls. Their commitment is hardly blind, however, because these people tend to see the problems of the organization more clearly than others. They have what poets call "negative capability," a quality that allows them to detach themselves from the craziness just a bit so they can maintain some sense of perspective (and some form of sanity). Sadly, the powers in the organization often take these people for granted. Their rewards often consist of more work or the pleasure of watching an up-and-coming hot shot take credit for what they have already done. At first glance, new leaders look at these quiet and unassuming people and see "dead weight"; after a few months, they learn that the "dead weight" is keeping the ship afloat. No matter how often their contributions are ignored, no matter how many insensitive and boorish leaders they have to suffer, they stay with the organization through it all. Some almost become martyrs, but most have too much self-confidence to debase themselves and too much good taste to become overly dramatic.

One can learn a lot from these people, who surely understand the meaning of grace under pressure. One can also learn from their co-workers on the other side of the fence, the people who have been there too long and should have moved on years ago. These are people who are fundamentally dissatisfied with their choice of occupation or organization but feel trapped, either by a lack of money or by a lack of confidence. They respond differently to crisis than the people in the core, often using it as an opportunity to prove the point that the organization is screwed up. Sometimes they get too abrasive and sometimes the self-pity is as thick as smoke, but when their sense of humor is in full operation, they can satirize the daily life of the company with the talent of Jonathan Swift. Many of them would like to approach their work with the same level of commitment as the people who form the core but have either been burned too many times or would much rather be somewhere else.

I would also say that most of the people who work in organizations are people you can trust. Oh, there are a few people who will disappoint you and there are enough jerks in any organization to make the experience quite unpleasant for the rest. The influence of the devious often outweighs the efforts of the straightforward, because people who choose to manipulate others can take advantage of honest souls who are only there to work. A bad leader can exploit good people by channeling their willingness to be helpful and responsive to toward achieving the leader's evil ends. These things do happen, and we will certainly go into them in more detail later in the book, but generally, the people you meet in organizations are decent human beings.

The advantages of sharing the organizational experience with people are best demonstrated by real-life stories that demonstrate how regular people cope with the difficult circumstances organizations too frequently create for them. I will now share a couple of those tales from my experience.

Story#1: Coming Together

I once supervised a group of quality assurance inspectors, made up of eighteen people spread out over three shifts. Our job was to inspect and test semiconductors before shipment.

I have to admit I didn't know a damned thing about semiconductors when I took this job. It was during a period in the history of Silicon Valley when anyone who had a degree was automatically designated a supervisor. That my degree was in English Literature with a minor in Asian Philosophy was irrelevant. They offered me a job as a supervisor and because there were no prospects for English teachers at the time and because I needed the money to help pay off a car I'd just purchased on one of those zero-money-down rip-offs for the underemployed, I grabbed it.

As it turned out, we became a very effective group. This was in part due to my willingness to let people make their own decisions, which had just as much to do with my ignorance as it did with any humanistic yearnings. There was also a curious norm of acceptance within the group that allowed a very diverse set of individuals to come together as a team. We had Koreans, Germans, Mexicans, African-Americans and American hill-billies. We had the young, the old and the middle-aged. We had country music fans and aficionados of the classics; we had some deeply religious people and some of the raunchiest people on earth. How they came together so cohesively is still something of a mystery to me. Perhaps because they knew they had freedom, they didn't feel the frustration that comes from feeling repressed; therefore, they had nothing to take out on each other. In the two years I supervised this group, they had their fights just like any family, but they never held resentments for long. They were there to do a job and because that job entailed cooperation with each other, they found a way to cooperate.

Our group was indispensable to the company at the end of every month, when we had to ship out enough semiconductors to make the monthly plan. As usually happens when an entire company is living from paycheck to paycheck, the entire process was chaotic. We didn't receive most of the chips until the last week, or more often the last day, of the shipping month. All hell usually broke loose, with the Production Control Manager constantly on the verge of a heart attack and the Production Manager threatening me with undefined yet dire consequences if we rejected any product (which we often did). The two of them would then find the responsible engineer and get him or her to sign a waiver to allow the product to ship. This was a predictable pattern for over two years at the time of the incident in question, providing everyone with the drama and excitement of naked human conflict.

This particular month, though, things were a bit slow. We kept waiting for the deluge and received only a trickle of product. I checked with the Production Control Manager who told me that because the overseas plants had failed to ship their product on time, this would be a relatively quiet month. It felt weird but at about 3:15 I went out and told the day shift that they could go home on time. Usually they wound up spending the night.

I went back to my office to engage in a leisurely chat with one of the engineers when the Production Control Manager showed up at my door, grasping his chest, face flushed, eyes ready to pop out of their sockets.

"A shipment (gasp) from Korea (wheeze) is coming in at midnight (gulp, gulp) and we've got to get it out!"

"Oh, shit!" I said, wondering what happened to cause such an unprecedented screw-up. Later I found out that some corporate VP was poring over the shipment numbers, found out that another division had fallen short and put the squeeze on the VP of our division to compensate. All sorts of macho threats and sentiments tumbled downhill in good hierarchical fashion, leaving our poor PC Manager within an inch of a coronary.

I knew that the PC Manager intended to dump the responsibility on my shoulders, so I did the first thing any manager does when faced with impending doom. I stalled for time. "Midnight!" I said. "But that means the shipments can't contribute to this month's revenue. Midnight starts a new month!"

The PC Manager looked at me with disgust, hardly concealing his disdain for my obvious lack of business savvy. "We can fix that," he said. "They've already alerted accounting that the month won't close until midnight Sunday. We've arranged with the shipper to do a special three o'clock pickup tomorrow afternoon. Now it's up to you."

"How much stuff are we talking about?" I asked.

"Over two million dollars." I didn't know how many semiconductors that represented, but I knew it was a hell of a lot of stuff, about a third of our total monthly shipments.

The PC Manager then left the premises for the bar across the street and a waiting tumbler of cheap bourbon. Meanwhile, I was moving into the second stage of management response: complete paralysis. I'd just sent the day shift home and the third shift was gone for the weekend. Only four of the eighteen inspectors worked swing shift, but they were all I had now, along with me. Even if we worked straight through, there was simply not enough time to get it done.

The third stage of management response to disaster is to panic and do whatever comes into one's head. What came into my head was to call everyone on the first and third shifts and ask them to come in and help.

Since I was never good at being a hard-ass, I posed my request very politely and made it clear there would be no repercussions if they had other plans. I'd learned two essential rules during my tenure as a supervisor: never mess with people's paychecks and never cancel their vacations. I felt this was close to violating rule number two, so I asked rather than demanded. There was probably a note of desperation in my voice that I was unable to filter out of the transmission.

"Here's the situation. I was just informed that there's a huge shipment coming in from Korea that will be here at midnight. If you can come in and help out, I'd really appreciate it, but if you can't or if you've made other plans, don't worry about it and I'll see you on Monday."

About half the messages were left on answering machines or given to adolescent children who were waiting for their parents to come home. Since there was nothing to do now but wait, I took off and went home to grab a quick nap and a shower. I got the shower, but the nap proved to be an impossibility. I kept thinking that I was going to be fired for failing to come through, for not having a backup plan in case of emergency, for letting everyone down. I drove back to work that Friday night believing my career was about to end before it began.

However, when I dragged myself onto the test floor about a half an hour before midnight, I was astonished to find everyone there. Every single employee on the first and third shifts had shown up and the second shift inspectors had all called home to say they'd be a little late. The group had even organized a potluck to get us through the ordeal. Some brought blankets and pillows in case someone needed to take a catnap in an unused office. Music was blaring from a portable stereo to help keep people awake.

I felt myself getting all teary as I stood in front of them. The only thing I could say was, "I love you people." And I really did.

Anyway, we pulled off the miracle, saved the Production Control Manager from bypass surgery and added a special war story to our collection. During our two years in business, we all drew closer to each other and spent a good portion of our off-hours hanging out together. The people in the group never hesitated to help each other out in time of personal need. When one of the inspectors went into the hospital, everyone paid a visit; when someone was having trouble with a kid or a spouse, someone else was always there to provide a shoulder to cry on. Sure, there were conflicts and competitions; there were complaints and arguments; there were screw-ups and inefficiencies. But all in all, this diverse group of quality assurance inspectors, representing various ethnic groups and lifestyles, became a family in the truest sense of the word.

And I still love those people.

Story#2: How to Survive When Your CEO Is an SOB

The second story involves an HR group I supervised a few years back.

At the time, the company I was working for was in the hands of a few very cynical people who believed that information was power and had no intention of sharing either unless it was absolutely necessary. Prior to the events in this story, these leaders had engaged in several questionable activities such as inflating revenue numbers, cooking the books and selling off profitable segments of the company to increase cash flow, all of which qualified them for huge bonuses from the parent company. The lack of ethical commitment was accompanied by a blatantly dictatorial management style that allowed no opening for reason. Sleaze permeated the company and we spent much of our time in human resources bailing managers out of trouble or trying to protect employees from various forms of psychological abuse.

You may wonder what on earth I was doing at such a regrettable institution. What I was doing was beating myself up for having made a stupid choice the year before. My desire for the position caused me to rationalize the inconsistencies in the organization that should have been danger signals. I wound up relocating my family and putting myself in a fragile economic position that would last for some time after accepting the job. In essence, I had let my desire for a leadership position, partially motivated by the "need" to show people in my life that I could "be someone," create a situation where I had lost most of my flexibility. My responsibilities to my children were too powerful to allow me just to walk out on principle. So I learned to live in the organization by biting my tongue and by attempting to reach a psychological compromise through doing whatever I could do to help people. What I learned is the importance of understanding the consequences of choices and resolved never to paint myself into a corner, trapped between responsibility to self and responsibility to others.

We will talk more about this balance in the second half of the book. Right now, let's just say I was a tortured soul but it was my own damned fault.

Despite the less than optimum environment, our little HR group had done very well. I had made the simple (and rather obvious) decision that the best contribution I could make was to tell my group to focus on doing what they wanted to do: help people. Since most HR people seek meaning in service to others, all I did by telling them to ignore the background noise and focus on service was give them a clear opportunity to do their jobs. We identified the things we could and couldn't do and focused on what we could do. If the company's management was going to create problems for its people, then we would help those people through those problems. This common focus allowed us to form a tight bond within the group, giving us a sense of purpose and unity that allowed us to survive random pay cuts, unexplained limitations on vacation usage and scads of other bad news announcements affecting the people we were trying to serve.

One afternoon one of the VP's called me into his office and gave me some astonishing news. He told me they had decided to close the entire manufacturing facility and relocate the operation to Mexico. He also informed me that the announcement would go out in less than forty-eight hours.

I had no inkling that this was coming (I told you they liked to play it close to the vest). I was the top HR executive—the only HR executive—and the people in charge had decided not to consult or involve me in a decision affecting a significant chunk of the workforce. However, our HR group was going to have to tell the people in manufacturing that they didn't have jobs in the middle of a recession when manufacturing positions were as rare as platinum.

This assignment unnerved me for personal reasons. I was close to the people in manufacturing. I had done employee relations there for a few years before moving into the director's role. We had been through a lot together and the people there trusted me to help them through anything, from getting their employment verifications through so they could qualify for a loan to helping them with personal problems to resolving conflicts with each other. They were a great group of people about to become victims of years of short-term thinking and irresponsible cost-cutting that had left us with a decaying manufacturing facility. The plant was out of date and I knew it; I also knew that it would have cost far more to upgrade the plant than open a new one across the border. The financial logic was inescapable (although that did not excuse the poor decision-making that resulted in the inevitable). What bothered me was that none of this was the fault of the people in manufacturing. They had done the best they could under increasingly difficult circumstances and now they were going to get the proverbial shaft.

My head was spinning as I left the office, partially filled with questions about plant closing regulations but largely crammed with the faces of the people who were going to feel the pain.

There was the ex-captain of the Cambodian army who had come over in the seventies, had found a job with our company and had years of perfect attendance. I asked him once what he liked about his job; he told me "they keep the building cool in the summer and warm in the winter."

There was the quiet little woman who had been there for ten or so years, keeping to herself and doing excellent work which few people noticed. I remembered when she lost her baby shortly after birth and the whole plant fell into a hush for about a week afterwards. When she had a healthy baby a couple of years later, they threw her the biggest baby shower in memory when she returned from maternity leave.

Then there was Billy Elmore. Billy was a scraggly young white guy with bad teeth and a helpless look on his face that made people feel sorry for him. Billy was the boy who always got into trouble, the only worker's comp case in history involving cat scratches (he'd gone out on break and tried to help a stray he'd found in one of the bushes). For years he had been holding onto his job by the thinnest of wires. Every month I helped his supervisor write warning letters on various infractions. However, he had always managed to pull himself back from the brink of disaster, though, leaving people to shake their heads and say, "that's Billy." Now his luck was about to run out. He was about to become a cost-cutting casualty and there wasn't anything he could do about it.

By the time I walked back to my office I was thoroughly disgusted. I was disgusted with myself for having taken this job and not having the financial resources to be able to tell them to stick it. I was disgusted with my superiors for giving me the opportunity to clean up another load of their bullshit. As I walked through the HR area, I could feel the people looking at me and I could tell from their faces that they were worried about what they saw in my face.

I went in my office and closed the door, something I never did. This probably alarmed them even more but I needed some space. Unfortunately, now their faces started to fill my mind and I thought about how I was going to break the news to them. Most of them were there because they cared about people. They did not want to become executioners. Although I had to live with my shortsightedness in accepting my job, I felt it was important to acknowledge to my staff that each of them had choices. Maybe I wasn't thinking like a good corporate citizen, but at that moment I felt a hell of a lot more loyalty to the human beings outside my door than I did to any damned corporation.

So, I jumped out of my seat, walked out of my office into the common area and shouted out, "Meeting!" We all gathered around the conference room table and sealed off the doors.

"I have an announcement. It has been decided to close down the manufacturing plant and move it to Tijuana. We've been charged with the responsibility to prepare the announcement, deliver it and implement whatever plan we come up with. We're looking at a gradual phase-out of operations over a period of nine months, so we have to figure out ways to keep people working here while they're setting up the Mexico facility."

I paused. I could tell from their faces that they were just as shocked as I was, but no one could think of anything to say. Naturally, they were thinking about their own mortality, as any human being does when someone else has to go.

I took a deep breath and continued. "Now on a personal note. I'm going to tell you what I really think. I don't know if this is the end of the bad news. I don't know what to think anymore. The executives are always looking for ways to cut costs and they're not too particular about where they cut. If it sounds like they can save money and not shoot themselves in the foot, they'll do it." I paused again. "That could mean us, too."

"So…if any of you want to start looking for another job, you have my support. You can take all the time you need to prepare resumes or go on interviews. I owe it to you for all you've done for me to tell you that I can't predict the future of this group or any other group in the company."

Someone asked, "What are you going to do?"

I sighed. "Right now I'm the sole support of two small children and I don't have the money to go without a job in the middle of a recession. I've got to stick it out. But that's my problem—you've got your own lives to think about."

There was a long silence. Then one of the group spoke up. "Those people need us. We've got to do whatever it takes to help them."

Suddenly the shock we had been feeling disappeared and we all rallied around those sentiments. By the time the meeting ended, we had a process in place that included outsourcing, resume preparation sessions, interview training, financial planning seminars and a communication plan that would give the manufacturing people all the information they would need to make the transition to new employment.

The plan turned out to be a very effective strategy for both the people losing their jobs and for the company as a whole. During the nine months of transition, only one person left the company early and we had no discipline problems of any kind. We helped the majority of people find work and we continued to help the others long after our official obligation to them had expired. By placing all our energy into living up to our responsibilities to our fellow human beings, we showed that the company still had a human face, which was a very important thing to communicate to the survivors. I justified our actions to the executives by telling them it would help the company avoid lawsuits and discrimination complaints (read: save money), which it did. We came out of the mess perfectly clean without a single legal tangle.

But that wasn't why we did it. At this point, none of us gave a damn about the company. We just wanted to help some people who were down on their luck.

Only one person out of the ten in my HR group left for another job after their captain told them that they should abandon ship. The person who left came back a year later once the company had gone through some positive changes and began moving in a more promising direction.

The experience of sticking together through tough times is something that happens to many groups that are part of organizations. We were a close-knit group to begin with, but the experience of choosing to stay together when all the evidence told us that we should split up was an extremely valuable learning experience for all of us. When the company finally did turn around under new leadership, we were ready for it. We shifted our efforts from resolving conflict and processing transactions to driving organizational change. The bad times had helped create a bond and the good times were ten times as enjoyable as the result of that struggle.

There is something about working in an organization that makes you want to stick it out. Part of it is you don't want to feel like you have wasted years of effort. Part of it is simple human stubbornness. But the main thing that welds people together during difficult times is the unique experience of going through those tough times together. This is what creates a cohesive community, and regardless of the pain we often have to endure to achieve that cohesion, the outcome often compensates us for our efforts by giving us that increasingly rare feeling of contributing to something greater than ourselves.

Rare indeed. The problems that beset corporations are unfortunately far more numerous than the joys of working in them. These problems form the basis of the next few chapters.

But before we dive into the muck and mire, take some time to consider your own experience by completing the following exercise in self-reflection.

*   *   *

Exercise 1: Discovering Motivations

Self-reflection is a key component of personal responsibility. We are going to practice this skill in several exercises. Use a notebook or computer to record your answers. If you opt for the low-tech approach, use a ring binder that allows you to insert pages.—In this first exercise, all you need to do is reflect on your motivations for having or wanting a job. Answer the following questions to get an idea of why you think you want a job.

1. List the things you want to gain from having a job (examples: financial security, respect, a good credit rating, etc.).
2. List the things you want to accomplish through your job (examples: achieve a particular vision, move ahead in an organization, practice artistry or craft, etc.).
3. Check which motivations for having a job appeal to you:
   —Earning money

—Providing continuity and stability to my life
—Building self-worth and self-confidence
—Contributing to and belonging to a community
—Meeting interesting people
—Other:—

4. Write down a few of the positive experiences you have had while working in an organization.

5. Review your experiences and look for common values that link those experiences. Write them down for these values are an important motivation for you in your work. (Example: in the two stories I told in this chapter, the common values were camaraderie and the ability to overcome obstacles).

THE RULES OF THE STATUS GAME

There are several futurists who have looked into their crystal balls and predicted the eventual demise of the hierarchy. The argument is that the good old chain-of-command is too burdensome, too sluggish and too inefficient to last in an age of warp speeds. Some have taken to putting their thoughts in the form of new organizational diagrams ranging from matrices to cloverleaves. The most peculiar variation is what is called the "upside-down organization," where the employees closest to the customer appear at the top of the chart. This is supposed to aid in the empowerment of employees, although in this case more power does not carry with it the inflated salaries reserved for the poor executives who find themselves on the bottom. Whatever the variation, whether you turn the organization upside down or inside out, the experts are telling us that the great movement of today is towards the flattening of the hierarchy. The era of massive corporate layoffs which continues into the present is a message that the power structure supports flattening, as thousands of former middle managers can corroborate. The hierarchy, proclaim the seers, is as dead as communism.

My response to this is simple: stuff and nonsense! You can take the hierarchy out of the organization but you will have a much harder time taking the hierarchy out of the people. You can doodle and play with new org charts all you want but it is a special talent of human beings to engage in one-upmanship or one-upwomanship. We create status hierarchies on the playground, in the gym, behind prison walls and especially in the workplace. All the systems thinking and diagrammatic creativity in the world will not change the elementary fact that human beings in groups will always seek their proper position in relation to others.

The last time I looked, America was still a society based on the questionable value of competition. We are obsessed with competition, as shown in our fixation with sports, with Nielsen ratings, with who's hot and who's not. A recent form of competition has appeared in the form of the daytime talk show, where average people reveal all sorts of embarrassing secrets about their personal lives in an attempt to outdo others in the game of seeing how far human beings will humiliate themselves for their fifteen minutes of fame. One reason why some people go into the business world in the first place is because they like the thrill of competition.

In organizations, competition appears in two forms. The first is the all-important desire to get ahead, to better one's financial position and perceived social value. The other form involves the simple human need for recognition, for attention, for validation of self-worth. It is sad that so many people in organizations feel horribly under-recognized to the point that they sometimes feel they have to screw other people to get the attention they feel they deserve, but such things do happen.

We value the home run hitter, not the league leader in sacrifice bunts. The quarterback is the one who gets all the endorsement contracts, not the poor bastards on the offensive line. For all the nonsense about teamwork spouted off in corporations, it is a very elusive reality. Individual recognition seems far more important to Americans than being an anonymous member of a team.

Still, it is interesting that many of the best experiences in organizations and many of the most memorable moments in one's working career happen as the result of people cooperating with one another. Perhaps this is because the experience is so rare. We are so used to the daily grind of political games that when people do get together to accomplish something, it is as exciting as winning the World Series. Unfortunately, many of these teamwork experiences are the result of crises created by status-obsessed executives who have been too busy playing politics to mind the store.

Let us never forget that it is impossible to analyze an organization independently of its culture. With that in mind, we must recall the words of Paul Fusell in the book *Class*:

> ...Alexis de Tocqueville put his finger precisely on the special problem of class aspiration here. "Nowhere," he wrote, "do citizens appear so insignificant as in a democratic nation." Nowhere, consequently, is there more strenuous effort to achieve—earn would probably not be the right word—significance. And still later in the nineteenth century, Walt Whitman, in Democratic Vistas (1871), perceived that in the United States, where the form of government promotes a condition (or at least an illusion) of uniformity among its citizens, one of the unique anxieties is going to be the constant struggle for individual self-respect based upon social approval. That is, where everybody is somebody, nobody is anybody.

American society is a place of constant competition for status, in the neighborhood or in the workplace. It is this all-powerful search for standing that pervades organizations and makes it more than naive to assume that hierarchies are ever going to go away. Even if your organizational chart shows a flat line, the people represented by that chart will create a hierarchy based on who is winning the status game.

Let's take a look at the rules of this always-interesting sport.

The Status of Knowledge

As noted in the previous chapter, information is power in the modern organization. Many people mine this vein for all it's worth.

The greatest power in an organization involves knowing something that another person doesn't know and letting them know that you know it. It would confer no status on you if you didn't let it slip that you are privy to inside information. Amateurs at the status game blow it every time by failing to keep the information a secret, their status plummeting with the words, "Okay, but you've got to promise you won't tell anyone else."

People take pride in what they know, which is why it is so difficult to teach them anything new. Where pride exists, arrogance is never far behind, and as we all know, arrogance is merely a mask for vulnerability. To put an adult in a situation where he or she does not know something, or where a lack of knowledge is exposed, is to put that adult through torturous embarrassment. It shows that you're not keeping up, that there is a possibility of being left behind and that your contribution will not be respected. For people with strong status needs, this is a direct threat to their existence.

Therefore, a basic strategy to maintaining status is a conservative approach to sharing information of all kinds. If you know something I don't know, you are more valuable than I am. I have to go through you to get something and it will always confer more status on you when you are in the role of dispenser of favors. People with specialized knowledge like programmers sometimes play this to the point of ridiculousness, which is why so many companies are frustrated with their information systems. You have to bow down to technical arrogance before you can get your E-mail to work properly.

Sometimes, though, this strategy backfires. When I was a QC Inspector on a graveyard shift, I worked with one woman who was the only person who knew how to run the Macrodata tester. Certain complex devices could only be tested on this machine, so she got to spend a lot of time working with higher-class engineers and technicians. She had the department supervisor in her back pocket, so he never pressed her about cross-training the other inspectors (and she certainly felt it was in her best interests to avoid doing so).

Unfortunately, one day a group of technicians came in and wheeled the Macrodata tester out of the lab. They had come up with a way to test the special devices on standard equipment and they didn't need the extra maintenance hassle and cost of running a separate machine. The protective inspector found herself the owner of now-worthless knowledge and with no status whatsoever. Since she didn't know how to do anything else and since she had convinced herself that doing what the rest of us were doing was beneath her, she had positioned herself right out of the company. She left for another job about two months later.

Strategic Communication

There is another problem in playing things too close to the vest: people will create rumors about you.

I think it was Rollo May who said that the primary cause of anxiety is a lack of information. If human beings lack information, they will just make it up to alleviate their anxiety. Truth is an insignificant consideration.

This presents a problem for someone who attempts to maintain status by being somewhat aloof. People love to tear down people in power positions (as we will explore in the chapter on leadership) and when they see someone acting as if he or she had pretensions to greatness, there is an irresistible urge to spread dirt about the inflated one. Sometimes this can become quite vicious, as powerless people who have failed at the status game can become deeply resentful of being labeled as know-nothing turds.

Therefore, people who are really good at the status game make sure they drop a little information now and then to those they consider beneath them who are likely to stir up trouble. These people are easy to identify, for they are usually very unhappy about their lives in general and very vocal about it. They have worked their way into higher status but still low-level positions, which gives them the right to bully lower status co-workers into submission and use those co-workers to vent their frustration about still being low-status in the overall scheme. If these people feel slighted by a presumed authority figure, that authority figure had better watch out.

Let's say you've just walked through a low-status work area with a lot on your mind and neglected to say hello and drop a few juicy tidbits to the people there.

Lower Co-Worker:	She really thinks she's something, doesn't she.
Loud and Unhappy:	She's not so hot. If she was, the guys would be all over her. You know, I've never seen her with a guy.
Lower Co-Worker:	*(responding to the cue in low-status agreement)* You're right. I haven't either.
Loud and Unhappy:	*(raises voice so others can hear, adds a note of astonishment to make it more realistic)* You mean Carolyn likes *girls*!—

Of course, if the company had a policy preventing discrimination on the basis of sexual orientation, the smear would fail, since Carolyn would have nothing to hide. In this case, if Carolyn were a lesbian, she would be better off to share the information openly, for that would raise her status by making her both "cutting edge" and a "protected class." The point is that if you want to win at the status game, you have to view all information as currency and learn to spend that currency strategically if you want to stay ahead of the plebeians who are ready to fall upon you with hungry mouths opened wide.

Long-Distance Communication

Another key to maintaining status involves placing as much distance as possible between yourself and the recipient of your message.

Distance increases status. If I avoid contact with you, I raise my status. This is why it is important to players of the status game to avoid face-to-face communication as much as possible. To communicate directly is to risk a fall from those hard-earned heights.

Executives who can closet themselves away in closed-door meetings and hide behind protective secretaries use this truth to great advantage. Still, people who are not endowed with the special privileges of rank can go a long way towards establishing distance between themselves and "undesirables." Here are some techniques people use to show others who their betters are:

Communicate Through Memo

Despite advances in technology, there is nothing like a coolly written memo to introduce a little formality into the mix. This is even more true when you can write the memo in pompous language and even better when you do not refer to yourself as the decision-maker.

Look at the following opening phrases and see if you can figure out which confers more status on the author:

> *"I have decided that..."*
> *"We have decided that..."*
> *"It has been decided that..."*

If you selected answer number three, score yourself a few bonus points. The first phrase is status-lowering because to display one's ego so ostentatiously in the first-person singular exposes one's insecurity. The second uses the "imperial we" and is therefore dated. The third is by far the best for generating distance, for human beings are not referred to at all. We have no idea "who" decided that, but it sounds ominous, as if this pronouncement was direct from the hands of God.

Use Technology to Raise Status

The development of voice and electronic mail virtually assures us a future in which we will never have to speak face-to-face to another human being again, thus avoiding the discomfort of direct communication. Some managers have worked this into an art form, delivering bad news through the magic of technology and making public appearances only when the political winds are favorable.

The great advantage of these technological wonders is that you can blast an adversary without having to stand there and listen to his response. I have worked in corporations where full-scale voice mail wars raged within their walls. The war starts with an apparently innocuous message containing an idea or suggestion to a person in another department. The recipient forwards the initial message to twenty other people after attaching introductory comments identifying the attached as something so completely stupid as to be beyond belief. The initial caller experiences outrage and flings a sarcastic response into the electronic ozone, making sure he has copied everyone in the listening audience. Alliances are formed and messages zoom back and forth over the wires, gathering as many attachments as the system permits, until all the mailboxes are full and people have to delete them to wage battle all over again.

Use Strategic Sarcasm

Whether communicating over voice mail or in those unpleasant circumstances where face-to-face communication is unavoidable, it is important to address your messages in tone of condescending sarcasm if you are serious about raising your status. This infuriates your opponents, which in turn lowers their status by showing them to be incapable of "handling it."

> *"Some people in this company don't seem to care about our customers."*
>
> *"You know, if you guys would spend a little more time working and a little less time socializing, you might be able to get things done."*
>
> *"It must be nice to have a real desk job, but there are some of us out here who have to work."*

The third statement is very effective for raising status because it lowers the opponent while sending the message that you are one hard-working SOB. Americans are suckers for ostentatious displays of the work ethic.

Leaders often use sarcasm in meetings to great effect, combining the power of authority with ridicule to destroy the credibility of the speaker. Some people I know were never able to recover their status after a few leader-initiated attacks in a public forum and had to leave their companies to seek credibility elsewhere.

Status Pockets and Stray Bullets

All organizations have status pockets that are roughly determined by organizational level. Because hierarchical level is generally accepted as an indicator of status, there are few status games that go on between the different levels beyond the common sniping at leaders that seems to be a human tradition. People tend to "know their place" and are content with taking a few potshots at their betters.

The really interesting status games occur when people are on the same level. This is because they are often in competition with each other for the next rung on the ladder. This simple fact can turn the nicest person into a shifty, devious backstabber who waits patiently for the opportunity to step over your cold body on the way to the top. Your relationship could stretch back as far as you can remember. You may have been through your shares of battles together and feel you have a bond as strong as SuperGlue. You may have even entertained this person at your home and rotated child pick-up duties. All of these considerations can vanish can in a moment if that person feels either a threat to their status or an opportunity to raise that status.

"I thought he was my friend," is the lament of the corporate jockey who has failed at the status game. What happened is that he or she has run up against a player who understands how the game is played. There are two basic rules for playing the status game successfully against your peers: deflect the stray bullet and step aside when the bullet is headed your way.

Deflect the Stray Bullet

The meeting starts and the boss is obviously looking for someone who can serve as a whipping post. He or she will fire a few warning shots in the form of sarcastic comments questioning the competence of his staff. "It would be nice if a few people around here cared about spending," or "I walked through your department the other day and I didn't see anybody working."

These are simply warm-up tosses. Status rules say you should hold your ground by remaining silent or saying something innocuous like, "I'll look into that." Although the latter comment appears to be status-lowering due to its essential wimpiness, it isn't. It simply confirms your lower status in relationship to your boss, which can help soothe the savage beast. Your peers won't see it as status-lowering because public ass-kissing is an acceptable strategy for people on the same organizational level. They do it, so it's okay for you to do it.

Step Aside When the Bullet is Headed Your Way

This is where much of the betrayal that takes place in organizations occurs. In this situation, the boss doesn't open with indirect sarcasm but a full-fledged attack. Victors in the status wars know that the thing to do is let someone else take the hit.

> Boss: *You were supposed to have that report on my desk Monday morning!*
>
> You: *Uh, I was waiting for the numbers from Finance.*

The Finance worker will probably be caught off-guard by the betrayal and begin to babble, which causes the boss to move in for the kill. His status is plummeting while your status is raised by the fact that his is on the slide. You have dodged the bullet and ensured that it is firmly planted in your co-worker's heart.

Be assured that if a bullet is headed your way, no one will step in front of you and save your ass. Your co-workers will gladly let you take the punishment, even if they think that what the boss is doing is unfair and unethical. They may even commiserate with you while standing over your body. This is because the need to maintain status is far more powerful in an organization than the need to do the right thing. No one ever gains anything by standing up for someone else, and if there is no gain, there is no action.

The single exception to this truth occurs when the boss is slipping in status and underlings feel more comfortable challenging his or her authority. This situation only happens when co-workers have inside information (conferred on them by a higher status individual) that the boss is on the way out. In this case, it isn't human kindness that gives someone the courage to take the bullet for you. It is the jockeying for position that inevitably occurs when there is something more to be gained—in this case, a promotion.

Status Through Stealth

While it may be hard to believe, there are people in organizations who seek status but have no interest in moving up the ladder. These folks have decided that competing for the next level is not their cup of tea, either due to self-doubt or a penetrating intelligence that has figured out that the desirability of a leadership position is highly overrated. However, these people are still hunting for status, albeit a status defined on their terms.

They want to be recognized for their hidden agendas, for the character they have chosen to play to validate worthiness.

There are several typical hidden agendas people use in organizations to confirm their own personal idea of status:

Poor Little Me: These are people who like to play victim. Their stories are full of abusive parents, abusive spouses, abusive bosses. All sorts of disasters befall them as they go through life lamenting, "nothing ever goes my way." The reward for this is that they receive attention and sympathy, which in turn gives them stories they can tell unappreciative family members about all the friends they have at work.

It's Not My Fault: While it is never good for your status to admit a mistake (people will gladly let you take the blame and the punishment), many people in organizations are terrified of the possibility that someone will suggest that they might have done something incorrectly. These folks are programmed to immediately deflect blame from themselves by revealing their fear so obviously that it makes the accuser back down to avoid getting caught in an interpersonal nightmare. "I didn't do it!" "I don't know anything about it." "I did the best I could—what are you going to do now?" These and similar statements are expressed in a louder-than-normal voice tinged with fear and anxiety, warning you that if you continue to press the attack you will feel guilty enough to crawl under a rock. By the way, people who combine "Poor Little Me" with "It's Not My Fault" are the people most likely to sue corporations.

Look What I Did: There are people in organizations who feel compelled to draw attention to their most trivial accomplishments. "See, I reorganized the filing cabinets for you!" "I sprayed Lysol on all the phones—it's the cold season, you know." "I looked into the possibility of multimedia training for you" (even though the thought had never crossed your mind). This agenda is usually directed at the boss, who in this case serves as the substitute for the parent who ignored the poor employee when he or she was a kid. It is often revealed by the attachment of that little phrase, "for you." You feel compelled to respond, "Oh, that's nice." If you ignore them or confront them on it, you are risking big trouble, for they may decide to go over your head for attention, dropping a few hints to your boss that you're an insensitive bastard and an ineffective leader. After all, you're messing with their status.

Territoriality

Another reason why the hierarchy will continue is the human instinct to establish territory. While we don't piss on cubicles to mark our spots, we do identify our boundaries in equally crude ways.

There seems to be no end to the willingness of people in organizations to engage in civil war. Most of the warring has to do with status. One reading of history could yield the interpretation that the Confederacy really went to war because the Union was treating them like low-status nonentities. Similar occurrences go on in organizations all the time, as if people were in constant watch for a Fort Sumter to give them an excuse to wage war to defend their inalienable right to feel self-important.

There are some basic tendencies regarding status and occupation that are permanent flash points ready to ignite into full-scale organizational war.

There will always be a conflict between salespeople and their counterparts in service and administration. Salespeople are rather ostentatious about the status symbols they collect: cell phones, awards, trips to the Caribbean. This offends lower level workers who make less money and can only dream about such things, content to spend their meager two weeks vacation camping at the nearest state park. Since salespeople are the purest manifestation of capitalistic greed in a corporation, a foreigner might wonder why the other money-worshipping Americans in the organization do not admire them. It's simple: if you've got it and you flaunt it, you're not a model of capitalism, you're an insensitive asshole rubbing my nose in my personal feelings of inadequacy. No American wants to know that there's someone out there better at getting things than they are.

In high-tech companies, salespeople are less important and therefore have less status than engineers and designers. I used to supervise a group that handled the processing of engineering documentation and I had a hard time getting my low-level workers to overcome their disgust with what they perceived to be raging arrogance. This is confirmed by the fact that those trained in technical subjects do not often communicate that they have much use for unpredictable and uncontrollable human beings. I once had an engineer in a communication class and was explaining to the participants why it was important to share one's thoughts and feelings with the other person to establish a human link. "Everything you're saying goes against everything I've learned!" he exclaimed. What often comes across as arrogance and superiority is a complete lack of interpersonal skills. When you add to this the money and perks thrown at them in a labor market crying out for technical expertise, you create a status conflict with unusual intensity. No matter how much I tried to point out an alternative view to my lower status group, they responded defensively and aggressively whenever an engineer entered the room. When the offending techie would leave, they would try to justify their existence by making self-serving comments to each other like, "If it wasn't for us, no one would test their damned products." This is similar to the lament of the admin groups who support sales: "If it weren't for us, they wouldn't get those fancy trips to Aruba." Both are the cries of people who know they have been one-upped in the status game and don't like it.

Of course, the status battle par excellence pits the people in the corporate office against those in remote locations like branches and operational sites. The corporate people have a serious advantage in that they have inside information or at least know how to act like they have it. The field people gain a bit by having the opportunity to complain about the endless stream of absurdities coming out of corporate, but they always wind up on the losing end of the status game. As we know, information is the currency of the modern organization and corporate people act like they own the bank. Of course, it is more likely that the corporate people know far less than they seem to know, but they know how to appear as if they are in on every decision. They also know that those people out there, no matter how close they are to the customer, are really unimportant because they are removed from the center of power. If this sounds like the bureaucratic arrogance we get coming from Washington, it's because the dynamics are precisely the same. Corporate people are expert at bureaucratic non-responses like, "because it's the policy," and "we'll get back to you on that" and "we're looking into that and will get back to you when we've made a decision." The "click" that often ends the conversation contains a message of its own, which reads, "You're an insignificant little ant and I am not required to pay any attention to you." The poor people in the field have to make things happen nonetheless, and although they're often very capable at doing that, they will never raise their status until they land a job at the corporate office.

In addition to the traditional conflicts between certain groups, people often make up their own territorial conflicts, based largely on the personality of their leaders. If an executive's peer has somehow embarrassed him or her in front of the boss or stepped aside when the bullet was coming, the troops below had better start digging in for a long campaign. I remember one marketing executive who conducted group meetings with his sales counterparts as if he were entering diplomatic negotiations with a sworn enemy. He would work out signals to his group beforehand, instructing them when to introduce certain pieces of information designed to scatter the opposition. If one of his subordinates veered from the plan of attack, he would kick them under the conference table! This guy may not a very good example because he was too obvious. What usually happens is that the troops get this uneasy feeling that they're being used for someone else's purposes and are not privy to the truth. I call this the "Vietnam Syndrome," for obvious reasons.

Even small-time operators can get into the territorial struggle for status. Office managers start rationing supplies and requiring people from other departments to submit two-page justifications for packages of Post-its. Human Resources people go around the company preaching policy, in part to attempt to control others (in the name of "protecting the company") but in large part to create a justifiable identity for a department in danger of being reorganized out of existence at any minute. Mail rooms and print shops become focused on departmental spending and controlling inventory not so they can become more efficient but because not having time for their internal customers raises their status. If I don't have time for you, I am implying that I am better than you are and that I certainly don't have to serve you. No wonder so many mailrooms and print shops are being outsourced to facilities management companies.

If you want to know whether a company you're planning to work for is a little version of the Balkans, go to their company picnic or Christmas party and pay attention to the seating patterns. If the vast majority of tables are occupied by people who belong to the same department and if the executive group is sitting up front surrounded by a network of tables containing smiling empty suits, then you had better become a status expert real quick.

The Status of Space

Once I was walking through the big open room where the company I worked for had stuffed all of the customer service, collections and other non-management (read: low status) groups. One wall of this room featured a huge electronic board showing how many customer calls were parked on the incoming lines. Usually this number was close to zero but on this particular day I noticed there were something like forty customers waiting in the queue. I looked around, saw about a dozen workers standing in and around one of the cubicles and sauntered over to see what was happening.

The center of attention was an employee who was wrapping up a tape measure. She saw me peeping through the crowd. "One foot," she said. "One foot?" I asked, confused. Did she want me to stand on one foot? Was I supposed to enter the cubicle hopping on one foot? She explained herself. "They got one more foot than we got," she intoned. I heard "tsks" and other sounds of disgust emanating from the crowd.

What had happened was that the company had recently moved the customer service people to a different location in the room. In building the cubicles, the facilities people had built the cubicles one foot wider than the cubicles for the collectors. The collectors were righteously pissed, as were the customers who were now on hold for twenty or so minutes. But the customers could wait. That one foot was an irresistibly attractive lightning rod for status discontent.

The meanings of space and status in organizations are hardly distinguishable. The more space you have, the more important you are. Executives have lots of space, clerical workers have a little space and if you're working in the mailroom you have no space. Status differences correlate exactly to the amount of space. Trappings clarify status differences when space is equal. A one hundred square foot office with a window is much higher in status than one with bare walls.

The one foot given the customer service people sent a message to the collectors that they were less important, which caused great discontent and a breakdown in customer service. When management heard about this disruption in the work environment, they wanted to fire everyone in sight, especially the ringleader holding the tape measure. "One foot— what's the big deal?" they huffed. However, since management had implemented the policies that clearly defined space limitations by salary grade level, there was little doubt as to who was truly guilty for the problem. Management had affirmed the value attached to space and it was patently unfair of them to blame their employees for following their lead and attaching high value to twelve inches of real estate.

Recent advances in office planning have given rise to the "open office" system where egalitarian values drive the architecture. In this system, everyone is out in the open and no one has an office. The entire workforce is divided into cubicles in an attempt to minimize status differences. Most people I have talked to despise open offices. This is not because open offices are bad in themselves, but because often a company's values do not suit an open environment where everyone feels free to talk. If a company changes to an open office set-up while still clinging on to other status-driven values such as limited sharing of information and internal competition, the atmosphere only worsens because nobody trusts anybody. People develop the annoying habit of whispering every sentence, even when what they are communicating is completely trivial. The constant sound of hushed voices leads a visitor to believe they have entered a spy novel or a modern version of the palace of Tsar Nicholas.

Go, Team!

Of course, corporations don't tell you that you're about to enter a world dominated by court intrigue. They tell you that you're part of a team!

Of all the clichés of corporate life, this notion of teamwork is the most worn. The word "team" has been so completely overused in corporate propaganda and by managers trying to "motivate" employees into doing what they don't want to do that it has lost any relevant meaning. The primary reason that teamwork has become such a pejorative word is that there are enough people in an organization who are in it totally for themselves and only care about the team long enough to pay lip service to it if that's what corporate standards of etiquette require.

It is a naive belief of many trainers and managers that organizational groups are like sports teams, or more accurately, idealized models of sports teams. I say idealized because the images presented are of mindless individuals who completely submerge themselves in pursuit of the group goal. This is obviously a myth created before the days of free agency.

Trainers and managers extend the myth to propagate the belief that on a team, everyone is supposed to cooperate with each other and each person is responsible for controlling their behavior to ensure that they don't do anything weird that interferes with the "team." Furthermore, they argue that each person on a team has something of value to contribute and each person's contribution is of equal value. I agree with the first part of the premise, but the second part is simply not true and is merely another example of human relations professionals trying to push consensus-building as the most desirable form of decision-making. The facts are very different. Teams can be successful with so-called "disruptive" influences and with superstars who are quite aware that they're more skilled than anyone else. The Chicago Bulls did quite nicely with as unique an individual as Dennis

Rodman and with as obvious a superstar as Michael Jordan. Let us not forget the Oakland A's of the 1970's, who fought with their owner and with each other on their way to three consecutive world championships.

I suspect that these efforts and management's support of superficial teamwork propaganda have much more to do with the desire to control individual behavior than with getting a group of people to work together to produce a commonly desired result. The best "teams" are those in which the leader focuses the group on a goal that the group already wants to achieve and then allows each person to contribute according to their abilities and personal styles without trying to stomp out any vestiges of individuality. Unfortunately, most corporations use the concept of team as a means of enforcing conformance and adherence to the company line. If someone fails to conform, all one has to do to put them in their place is to say, "he's not a team player."

Another tip: if you go to your interview and all you hear is the old "we're a team" line, politely decline the offer by stating that you would prefer to work for an organization that permits people to work intelligently together.

Still another tip: if in your interview you hear the recruiter extolling the egalitarian nature of the organization as evidenced by its casual dress code, the recruiter is probably an idiot. Anyone who has spent any waking hours in America in the last few years understands that there is more status attached to the brand of tennis shoe you are wearing than to a double-breasted suit.

Hierarchies and Social Order

As I said in the beginning of this chapter, hierarchies may disappear from the drawing boards of organizational development consultants but people will always create them nonetheless. This is not necessarily a bad thing. It is reflected in the common wisdom of "too many cooks will spoil the broth." Fusell quotes the more pointed remark of Oscar Wilde: "the brotherhood of man is not a mere poet's dream: it is a depressing and humiliating reality." There are many reasons why communism didn't work but the basic tenet of a Utopia of "each according to his needs" is simply not in keeping with either the reality of human pettiness or the everlasting drive for individual distinction.

After all, hierarchies have produced great things. NASA put Armstrong on the moon; the old railroad companies linked the nation. On the other hand, hierarchies also sanction astonishing acts of cruelty and give license to outrageous pomposity. It is rare to find a hierarchy structured around competence like those we see on *Star Trek*, but a few do exist. The reason more do not exist is that hierarchies assume that competence is a fixed asset that never changes. This goes against the reality of human limitations: hitters go through hot streaks and hitters go through slumps. To assume that the person on the top is going to be the right person to lead an organization through every crisis is unrealistic. The answer is no doubt a form of leadership that allows the hierarchy to shift according to the needs of the moment, so that power is distributed to the people who are best able to lead the organization through a particular crisis.

However, this is not going to happen any time soon, for once people have attained a position of power and status, it is extremely difficult to give it up. We are basically insecure about our status and the loss of that commodity is a frightening prospect. Our mythos is oriented in one direction—up—and the possibility of "down" is something we fervently wish to deny.

This habit of denial also manifests itself in the second major problem in today's corporation, which has to do with the issue of control.

*   *   *

Exercise 2: Looking at Status

While we can all laugh at the silliness that goes on in a company when people try to establish a pecking order, we have to remember that we are part of the silliness as well. Everyone in an organization participates in status games to some degree whether they want to or not. It is part of what you have to do to survive in a hierarchy.

This exercise will look at your particular organization's rules about status as well your own orientation to the subject of status. Record your answers in your notebook.

1. How does your organization define status? What gives someone status in your organization?
    —Knowledge
    —Strategic Communication
    —Long-distance Communication
    —Organizational Level
    —Profession (type of occupation)
    —Territory (certain departments may have higher status)
    —Participating on the "team"
    —Other:

2. How do you define high status? What in your opinion gives a person greater status?

3. How do you define low status? What in your opinion gives a person lower status? (Hint: It might help if you started your thinking with "I would never be caught dead doing X" and then filling the blank with your response.)

4. What status games do you find yourself playing in the workplace? Be honest and forgive yourself in advance.

5. What do you think motivates you to play the status game? (Hint: go back to your answers in Exercise 1 and look at your motivations for working).

THE CORPORATE CONTROL FETISH

Most organizations invest as much money and energy into controlling the people who work for them as they do in delivering their products or services. This is accomplished through various means, from policies to procedures, from mission statements to the concept of professionalism, from guilt trips to subtle threats. As corporations have matured over the years, the subtle approach has become the preferred method of keeping people in line, for it is considered less crude than those associated with the traditional chain-of-command. This is the direct result of managers attending management development seminars that are devoted to learning how to manipulate people so they will be more likely to do what they want them to do.

However, control is still control, no matter what you do to gussy it up, and there is no doubt about it: management is still in control of today's organization. All that has been written about empowerment and workplace democracy has not changed the fact that you do not have much of a say as to whether or not you will keep your job if there is to be a layoff. People can still be fired for insubordination, even in our enlightened age, even though the word "insubordination" has been supplanted by the politically correct "failure to follow reasonable instructions of a management representative." Nearly every company has a policy reminding you that employment is "at will," and although the phrase is really only there to protect the collective behinds of the people in charge, the message is clear. The real bottom line for you is that management has the power to decide the course of your financial future. The general anxiety about job security in today's environment has only strengthened management power, for if people are insecure, they are much less likely to challenge the way things are.

We will note two important points before proceeding. The first is that on the whole, most people in the workforce do not object to being controlled. The human preference for order over chaos is part of the reason for this, but the greater part has to do with the learned helplessness of the American workforce. Few believe they can change the status quo, so they "learn to live with it." The second point is that there are several perfectly rational reasons why organizations implement controls, as does any other community populated by human beings. All communities work to protect their interests, and in this regard, corporations are no different. Rules forbidding the theft of trade secrets, for example, are both rational and essential given the dynamics of an often cutthroat marketplace.

Unfortunately, most organizations go far beyond what is rational in implementing rules, often displaying the type of paranoia that Andy Grove says is so essential to survival. In the sense that there are people out there deliberately trying to screw organizations, Mr. Grove's wisdom is correct. The current legal environment has provided opportunities for many a con artist to go after companies with deep pockets. Still, the excessive controls on human behavior spawned by the terror of lawsuits and accompanying bad press are a good example of punishing the vast majority of one's workforce because of a few bad apples.

We repeat that one cannot analyze an organization independently of its culture. The resort to the lawsuit to resolve problems in our society is a cultural sickness and as such, corporations are merely victims of a social disease. The fact that all an employee has to do is threaten a lawsuit to get some kind of settlement from a corporation is not entirely the fault of the corporation. The corporation is just caught in the game like everyone else. It is a web that begins with well-intentioned but poorly written legislation which is in turn exploited by unethical lawyers and their irresponsible clients, which in turn makes it seem sensible for organizations to implement severe restrictions on human action. It is a sad state of affairs, indeed, for my experience tells me that the people who are really victims of discrimination or harassment rarely file lawsuits because they do not want to involve themselves in what is essentially a dehumanizing process. Ineffective managers who avoid problems are promoted while the poor stiff who confronts an employee on a performance problem winds up on the witness stand with the broiler set to maximum. These are all symptoms of a complex cultural problem involving the nature of responsibility, which we will address later.

But beyond the controls implemented in an attempt to deal with a bad situation, working for any organization, be it corporate, government or non-profit, means working within certain limitations on human action. The bottom line is that if you are a reasonably creative person, if you value spontaneity, if you find it difficult to control your human need to eat, drink or go to the bathroom, if you like to dress as you please and come and go as you like, then stay the hell away from organizations.

Policies and Procedures

Most people in organizations complain about procedures and red tape. Having been in charge of departments (a Specification Center and a Human Resources Department) who contributed greatly to the procedural muck, I can certify that people have a legitimate complaint. Most procedures are completely unnecessary and designed to frustrate productivity rather than enhance it. Some even cross the line into the absurd. One company I know created a flow chart and procedure for making coffee (and the result was hardly Starbucks, let me tell you).

One sort of procedure is the "operator instruction document," which tells the employee step-by-step how they are to perform certain aspects of the job. The reason for having such a procedure is to attempt to enforce consistency. Consistency is important to management because they generally value efficiency, which enhances productivity, which finally translates into money in the bank. What is rarely if ever considered is the effect of consistency on the human beings charged with implementing the procedure. Having to do the same thing over and over again in exactly the same way may improve efficiency and may enhance quality but it dulls the spirits of those assigned to the task. It also reduces the threat that a low-level employee will come up with a better way of doing things, heaven forbid. Organizations implement procedures to ensure efficiency but always neglect the reality that turning people into virtual robots is a dehumanizing act.

Thank God for the human spirit, though, since most operator instruction procedures are never implemented in the fashion intended by the designers. Most people I've worked with, be they on the manufacturing floor or in the professional cubicles, don't even bother to look at the procedures or flow charts, preferring instead to do things their own way. Most procedures and flow charts are not designed to cope with the variables of a chaotic environment, so people often need to ignore them to get the job done.

However, those same people who ignore procedures governing their own jobs will turn into bureaucratic statues when equipped with a procedure that can stop an enemy from another department dead in their tracks. "I'm sorry, we can't do that, it's the policy," is still an effective and frequently used means of defending against invaders. In this case, procedures become a way to control through status, for you can always raise your status when you can frustrate the advances of your opponent. "It's not in the policy" is the organizational linguistic equivalent of "stick it up your ass."

However, the human spirit, with its need to manifest independence, comes to the rescue once again. People who are frustrated by the procedures that another department is using to block their march towards progress are incredibly creative at going around the system to solve their problems. When I ran a Human Resources Department, the managers amazed me with their innate ability to work around the bullshit we were throwing at them. I finally got fed up with it and threw out most of the policies, replacing them with value statements that allowed us to exercise judgment instead of trying to control people by quoting rule, chapter and verse. We removed the status motive from the picture and began to work with managers instead of being at war with them all the time.

For some organizations, though, such an approach would be heresy. There would be lawyers and professional experts screaming about the risks of abandoning policies (although you could probably find an equal number of attorneys arguing just as persuasively to get rid of the polices if no one follows them anyway). There are many people in the more traditional organizations who have built their careers on knowing internal procedures, and to ask these people to think for a change would probably send them into catatonic shock. Organizations who have fully embraced quality programs or who are flowcharting everything in sight in order to re-engineer people out of existence would be appalled by the thought that one can do quite nicely without written procedures. Methinks the fact that they protest too much means that the people who want to protect the existence of policy are concerned with something other than safeguarding the interests of the organization. Policy and procedure owe their existence to habit and the fetish for order and not to the need for protection.

This is not to say that all policies are unnecessary. Some policies such as equal employment opportunity policies are essential because organizations need them in writing to make the government happy if they ever get audited. Other policies are designed to adhere to FASB requirements or ISO 9000 rules while others are written to fulfill the intent of safety-related legislation. The common element in all compliance-based policies is that no one in the organization ever reads them, written as they are in pompous formal English reminiscent of Milton's essays or the zoological passages in *Moby Dick*. These policies are mere window-dressing, empty pages designed to please outside authorities that often lack meaning for the people inside the organization. They are necessary because they provide the outside world with the appearance of compliance with the social or business standards. They are not important in a real operational sense.

The truly important procedures are rarely written down because they are the procedures used by executives, who don't like anything written down and published if they can help it. The advantage of unwritten procedures emanating from above is that you can again control people through status, which is something people rarely question. People may argue about paragraph 3.11 on the seventy-second page of the operator instruction document dealing with how to properly clean the PC board tester, but they cannot question what is not on paper and rarely challenge authority.

One executive I know had three important procedures for controlling expenses in the company. First, he made sure that he never carried a pen so that he would never have to sign anything; all he had to do is say, "I don't have a pen" and slip away before a subordinate could produce one. Second, he dealt with requests for expenditures by placing them in a file folder on his desk without looking at them. He would then wait a couple of weeks and if no one asked about them, he would just toss them in the trash. Since he maintained a status distance from his subordinates, they rarely entered his office, and he made sure that he remained invisible enough so that no one could find him to ask about their request. If by chance a subordinate confronted him, he would say the request must have been lost in the mail and tell the subordinate to resubmit it. He knew that the subordinate would often forget to do so unless it was vitally important. Finally, if he received the second request, he would sign it, confident that the expenditure was worthwhile. The result of all this sleight-of-hand was that expenses were under control, money was set aside to deal with the demands of an unpredictable CEO, and the Finance Officer looked like a responsive and loyal team player.

This Finance Officer was unusual only in the degree of personal control he exercised over expenditures. Most corporations use something called "the budget process" to keep expenses in line. The rules governing the budget process create a great deal of confusion in corporations, particularly for new managers. In fact, there are only two basic rules. Rule number one: if the money you need is not in the budget, you can't spend it. Rule number two: even if the money you need is in the budget, you can't spend it. Spending in a corporation has more to do with the current mood of the executive team than financial objectivity, which means that budgets, like many leaders, exist only to stop progress, not to achieve it.

We will close this section with news of a recent development taking place in some organizations bitten by the cost-cutting bug. These are policies that discourage celebrations and holiday gatherings on "company time." It seems as if some organizations believe that birthdays and holidays should not exist, as if their new model of leadership is Ebenezer Scrooge. Employee birthdays are now relegated to the 15-minute afternoon break period. Valentine's Day is out; Halloween is still somewhat in, largely involving workers in the lower rungs who have less status to lose by dressing in costume than their stiffer cousins in upper management.

Even Christmas is now an opportunity for corporations to save money. One organization I know used to have managers hand out turkeys to every employee during the holiday season. They changed this policy to eliminate the costs of lost management time and turkey transport by sending the employees equivalent-value gift certificates in the company mail. The employees raised a stink about the whole thing, using the new policy as evidence that management did not care enough about them to wish them a happy holiday face-to-face. The company then turned the tables by using the complaints from the ungrateful bastards to eliminate the Christmas gift altogether. Now the employees get nothing at all.

You see, when executives (who are human beings just like you and me) spend money they expect to get something in return—in this case, appreciation, loyalty and happy faces. They become very resentful when their gifts and generous gestures are not well received. One executive I know was so enraged by rumors that some people were not planning to show up at a Christmas party scheduled during company hours that he put out a policy threatening to fire any employee who failed to attend.

And a happy holiday to you, too.

Professionalism

One of the most powerful forms of control exerted in any organization is the phenomenon called "professionalism."

What gives professionalism its awesome power is that no one can define with any precision what it is. In some organizations, it means men wearing suits and women wearing dresses. In other workplaces, such fashion would represent an anachronism. Sometimes professionalism means not disagreeing with anyone publicly, whereas in other organizations, such a norm would be considered unhealthy. We can definitely say that anything that is also considered a social taboo or a breach of etiquette such as farting in a closed-door meeting would fall under the category of "unprofessional," but beyond the obvious faux pas, professionalism seems to be whatever those in power decide it should be.

It is critical that anyone deciding whether or not to take a job do as much digging as possible to find out what code of professionalism exists in the organization before considering employment. Much of the dissatisfaction stemming from a feeling of "I don't belong here" has its origin in working for a company whose definition of professionalism is out of sync with the employee's definition.

Let me give you some examples. I once worked for a company in Silicon Valley, sharing a large office with four other people. Whenever we wanted to toss an idea around in the group, we would simultaneously toss a Nerf football to each other. This helped us to relax and to think more creatively. No one in the company ever accused us of unprofessional behavior. In fact, after a reorganization left me with a new boss, he happened to walk in while we were throwing the football and instead of clamping down on our childishness, held his hands out to receive a pass. The organization permitted play because it perceived it as a necessary form of release in a highly stressful environment. None of this gaiety affected our performance one iota. We always got the job done.

However, I left this playful environment for an easier commute and a change of careers. This turned out to be a mistake because I neglected to learn what the new organization meant by "professional behavior." Footballs were definitely out, despite the fact that there were no company rules specifically prohibiting the launching of projectiles on company property. It was obvious that playfulness was not at all valued in this environment just by the feel of the place. These people meant business! The only input permitted in meetings had to be either factual or rational, which not only makes for a very long meeting but also wipes out the possibility of any creative thinking whatsoever. Whenever the tension of the inherent boredom was too much, little signs of playfulness like small jokes and witty repartee would sprout up, only to be crushed as the chairperson cleared his or her throat to get "back to business." I should have listened more carefully to the language the recruiters used during the interviews, for I realize now that it was smooth, polished and completely devoid of any originality or emotion. These people had stuffed their humanity where the sun didn't shine and worked under the belief that a professional environment means a serious, deadly dull and ordered existence free from surprises, mirth and any expression of feeling.

Often, any expression of emotion is classified as "unprofessional" by many organizations. Getting angry—I mean, really getting angry, as in shouting and pounding the table and punching walls—is generally considered unprofessional, although executives get away with it because of their status. On the other side, having too much fun is often considered unprofessional, especially in companies afflicted with what C. W. Metcalf calls "terminal professionalism." Crying is definitely considered bad form, whether you are male or female. Once I was helping a manager decide how to approach an employee on a performance problem, telling him that once he delivered the bad news he should sit there patiently and allow the employee to express her emotions. He exclaimed, "Can't I make her leave the office if she starts crying—you know, until she can pull herself together?" This manager, like so many other managers I've worked with, considered confrontation with a normal human feeling such a terrifying prospect that he put off dealing with the performance problem altogether.

As with emotion, certain basic human activities are often no-nos in the workplace. Obviously, any kind of sexual expression is definitely out. Legal developments have forced employees to take down their Brad Pitt and Salma Hayek pinups and to pursue romantic relationships with a stealth and secrecy similar to that of Winston Smith and Julia in Orwell's *1984*. Sleeping on the job is definitely considered bad form, even though nearly everyone working would love to take a little nap right after lunch. Spending too much time in the bathroom is a bad thing, especially for lower-level non-exempt employees who have to account for every minute of their working day due to antiquated wage-hour laws and supervisors operating under the ancient dogma of "time is money." Eating and drinking at one's workstation is often forbidden, though this prohibition is enforced more religiously at the lower levels of an organization. Although it is perfectly rational to forbid eating and drinking in a clean room environment or to ask employees working in a clothing store to avoid spilling crumbs on the merchandise, some organizations go far beyond the need to protect product or equipment in implementing anti-consumption rules. I know of one employee who was given a written warning for being unprofessional by eating at her desk even though she never saw a customer and was so overworked by her poorly-organized boss that she had to either eat at her desk or face the possibility of starvation.

Standards of professionalism also vary according to the occupation. Engineers and programmers have the loosest interpretation and companies give them more slack because everyone thinks they're a little crazy anyway. Sales and marketing types have the greatest limitations, both because of the required "Dress for Success" look and the need to engage in small talk that assists them through the networking process. Their compensation for having to work under strict professional standards is the annual convention where they are permitted to release their repressed feelings in drunken orgies. Finance and administration groups contain the most conservative and reserved version of the professional while manufacturing groups rarely enter into the discussion, since manual labor is often considered outside the realm of "professional." Having worked with or within all the functions in an organization, though, manufacturing groups are usually the most enjoyable, for the simple reason that the code of professionalism does not penetrate far enough into the manufacturing plant to suppress the human element.

It's too bad that most of them are being shipped off to Mexico and Southeast Asia.

Assimilation by the Collective

Everyone who is familiar with *Star Trek* knows about the Borg. They are a civilization of cybernetic beings who assimilate other species into a collective. Borg have no individuality whatsoever. They think and act collectively, limiting their communication with other species to a few pithy slogans such as "resistance is futile." There is no conflict within the collective and everyone is literally on the same program.

Like many corporations, they have a vision!

Now I should state up front that I am a firm believer in mission statements. I believe any organization should have a statement of intention to define its activities and give them focus. A good mission statement embodies what the organization stands for and what it hopes to achieve, giving everyone involved, be they shareholders or employees, the opportunity to join the cause if those values and intentions coincide with their own. I can read Ben & Jerry's mission statement and decide if making the finest quality all natural ice cream for a community-conscious company is something that fills me with passion or is a worthy enough cause to give them my investment dollars to create more gallons of New York Super Fudge Chunk.

If that were the only reason organizations create mission statements, the world would be perfect. Unfortunately, many feel the need to indoctrinate their people with the vision in an attempt to turn them into Borg, who are much easier to control than free spirits.

I once worked for a company that got religious about quality. Everyone had to go to quality school. Everyone in had to read a particular book that explained and expounded upon the new company philosophy. Managers began communicating entirely in stock phrases borrowed from the book, as if they were stuck on a tape loop. The final phase of indoctrination involved "asking" all 10,000 employees to sign their names on a "quality pledge" blown up into large posters. We had a big party with free food (the most effective way in the known universe to induce compliance) and everyone in the crowd, under intense peer pressure and under the watchful eye of management, "voluntarily" pledged their lives to the pursuit of quality product.

I was not surprised when the company went through massive layoffs and was finally split up and bought out by a number of different institutions about five years later. In their religious fervor, the people behind the program had forgotten that any organization has to maintain a certain amount of disorganization to survive. Without it, organizations become victims of dogma and process. They fail to see new business opportunities when they arise because they have learned to think and perceive in only one mode. Their employees stop all attempts at innovation because they know the organization cares more about compliance than creativity. Everyone becomes a convert to the program and the organization dies a slow death because they have forgotten how to improvise in the face of changing circumstances. I remember someone saying at the time that they had taken all the fun out of the organization. The executives had the satisfaction of looking at all those signatures on the wall, and may have even deluded themselves into believing that the signatures represented real commitment. What they were really seeing were the signatures of people who were as dead as the people on the voting lists of Chicago in 1960. In achieving control, they had wiped out the possibility that people could actually enjoy working there and use their own motivation to move the company forward.

There are other organizations that are big on the word "commitment." They'll sponsor revival meetings where people stand up in front of the group (under not so gentle prodding from priest-facilitators) and tell what they are going to do to demonstrate their commitment to the vision. People comply and the priest-facilitators go away thinking they have really done a good job "moving the vision forward." Behind their backs, people talk about what bullshit the whole thing is and prepare to leave the company in droves.

Corporate America can get away with this kind of mass indoctrination because they are not subject to the Bill of Rights. This surprises most people, who no doubt slept through civics class. The Constitution is concerned with government, not private institutions, and as such, the catch-phrase is always "The Government shall make no laws". This means that corporations can certainly restrict any of what the average American thought were inalienable rights, which in turn means that one has a limited number of options when faced with the need to comply to corporate demands. If you speak out, you are often branded an outcast and subtly excluded from participating in decisions or receiving promotional opportunities. Most people go along with such programs publicly (one of those "trade-offs") and make jokes about it in the lunchroom to compensate.

This is not, by the way, an argument for more democratic institutions. The reason why corporations can restrict rights is that they need to be efficient in a competitive marketplace. Democracies are notoriously inefficient and given the recent record of voting in America, both in terms of the level of participation and the quality of the results we see in Congress, I am not sure I would want to turn over decision-making in the company to the masses. Democracy in the workplace is a wonderful concept, but until the people in power are willing to share the information that will enable people to make intelligent choices and until the people doing the work are willing to accept the responsibility that comes with the freedom to choose, it is not a feasible idea.

But it is equally true that fascism is not a feasible idea either, and the desire to get everyone "on the same page" is often taken to the extreme. Often born in the passion or tremendous insecurity of the CEO, the push to get everyone in line with the vision often becomes a war of attrition in which the survivors are empty-headed drones content to follow the rules. The creative, the talented and those with intelligence and the capacity for critical thought leave such brainwashed organizations for freer climates.

If they stay in organizations at all.

Planning, Performance and Other Myths

Truly anal organizations take the company vision and break it down into goals and objectives for each person in the system, moving down through the hierarchy until they are satisfied that everyone knows their place. The astonishingly naive people behind such programs believe that when everything is perfectly organized, the organization will achieve its vision and everyone will ride smiling (professionally, of course) into the bright new future.

This notion is so silly that it defies belief. Thank God these people were not in charge of the European Theater in World War II: Patton would have stalled long before his supplies ran out and The Battle of the Bulge would have required several unproductive meetings to discover why the Germans weren't behaving according to the plan. We were much better served by a leader like Dwight D. Eisenhower, who observed, "plans are useless but planning is indispensable."

What Eisenhower was getting at is that thinking about the future and possible scenarios is an effective mental discipline that can help prepare people not just for the most likely eventualities but all eventualities. Planning is not a method of controlling human behavior but a thought-provoking process designed to increase an organization's ability to respond to both the expected and the unexpected.

The world of commerce is changing so quickly now that no one is really certain of the future or what to make of much that is going on in the present. If you've paid any attention to the experts who have tried to predict the behavior of the stock market in the past few years, it is obvious that they don't have the slightest idea what they're talking about. The key to success, therefore, is not necessarily to increase an organization's ability to predict the future (which predictions are invariably wrong) but to develop an organization's ability to improvise according to changing realities. Predicting the future is a sound exercise, though, for it prepares the people in the organization for uncertainty by awakening their minds to new possibilities.

Most corporations, however, do everything possible to prevent their people from developing their abilities to improvise, to respond to new information or to innovate. Companies that are Borg-ifying their populations cannot process information that contradicts the dogma in their mission statements. Strict notions of professionalism wipe out the ability of people to be playful, an essential prerequisite to creative thinking. Job descriptions and annual performance objectives limit the ability of people to respond to the inevitable developments that fall between organizational cracks and outside the yearly planning cycle. Spontaneity is discouraged because when people are truly spontaneous, they tend to drag up things from their subconscious like sexual imagery and weird thoughts that are not only considered unprofessional but can get the organization into legal trouble.

I once worked with an organization whose leader was keen on translating the vision into individual performance objectives for everyone in the company. We implemented the vision but there were various delays in implementing performance plans. People were stalling and he wanted to know why. I had to tell him that the reason they were stalling is that people were pursuing new business opportunities and trying to meet changing customer needs and simply didn't have the time to translate their activities into objectives that they felt would be obsolete within a month. Ironically, the organization was meeting most of the executive's goals in cost reduction, in new business and even in developing their people. The people working for him didn't need individual performance objectives because they understood the vision and had enough native intelligence to figure out how to do that all by themselves.

Some will argue that a company must have job descriptions and performance objectives so they can compensate people fairly. After all, you want to reward the people who are doing the work by giving them good raises and punish those who are not by giving them lousy raises.

There are two fallacies in this line of thinking.

In the first place, all work in organizations is of a cooperative nature. You can't get anything done in any organization all by yourself. You have to gain the cooperation of the people above, below and around you to make anything happen. This is even more true in a hierarchy, where functions are structured according to specialization. While we can argue that organizations should not be structured in such an obviously restrictive manner, that's the way things are, and because of it, all work in an organization is by necessity, teamwork. We resist this notion because it collides with good old-fashioned American individualism, but the fact is that even history's heroes had a whole lot of faceless people behind them to help them reach hero status. Neil Armstrong couldn't have walked on the moon without a little help down below. Compensating people solely for individual performance is an act devoid of reality.

The second fallacy lies in the way compensation is determined. Generally, a job's worth is decided by the general labor market, as revealed in salary surveys collected by the Human Resources Department. What this means is that a lazy programmer who contributes nothing to an organization can make four times as much as the lowly administrator who saves the organization's ass day in and day out. In other words, what a person is paid may have no connection whatsoever to what they contribute, but is more closely related to having a job valued in the general labor market.

Aha, goes the counter-argument, the reason you have performance objectives is so that if the programmer is not hitting the goals, you can get rid of him. I will respond by saying what everyone already knows: people rarely get fired for performance in any organization. The termination process is always a drawn-out affair, punctuated by conflict and inundated with documentation. People who are intelligent enough to be programmers can inundate a naive HR person with enough technical bullshit as to leave the matter of performance completely unclear, thus ensuring survival.

The problem of compensation and performance in corporations today is a small symptom of a larger social problem. America is a society that pays mediocre relief pitchers millions and its teachers, law enforcement officers, social workers and artists next to nothing. Our culture has completely disconnected reward not only from effort and results, but from basic values as well. Organizations suffer from the general confusion surrounding these issues, but aggravate the problem by implementing fruitless controls in the name of performance planning.

Cause and Effect

One must wonder why organizations go through so much effort to control their members. After all, these are generally intelligent and decent people who are otherwise permitted to exercise such weighty responsibilities as raising children and voting in a democracy. It is certainly not in the best interests of the membership to inflict damage on their organization. So why bother to exercise so much control over reasonable people who do not pose much of a threat and are fearful enough just to be thankful to have a job at all?

One reason is that those at the top feel they are in an extremely vulnerable position, given the challenging task of trying to satisfy shareholders, regulators, customers and employees. When one feels vulnerable, one turns to arrogance to mask the vulnerability. Arrogance works on the sad belief that "what you control cannot hurt you." Therefore, many of the controls implemented by organizations are designed to protect leaders from threats, real or imagined, to their power and authority. Controls then become a means to reinforce the hierarchy, which is silly, since most people accept the hierarchy as being in the nature of things.

But controls also exist because leaders feel responsible for the health of the organization. Threats to organizational health in the form of disgruntled employees are real concerns. There are people who join organizations solely for their own self-interest, who exploit companies for money, training or experience and have no intention of contributing beyond the minimum necessary to keep the job. There are also people with needs for personal glory out of sync with the company's direction or its financial reality. These people waste everyone's time and money implementing grandiose but fundamentally flawed projects that live on in the form of unsolvable problems long after they have moved on. Finally, for the vast majority of people who work in organizations, the job they hold was not their first choice for their life's work and so they maintain a psychological distance from true involvement. Leaders never really know when people are going to bail out and leave them with a real mess on their hands.

The problem is a never-ending cycle, for most employees would not be disgruntled if they felt they were treated with respect and shown confidence in their abilities. We will come back to the question of leadership in a later chapter, but for now we must explore a deeper problem that creates many of the never-ending cycles and much of the absurdity we experience in organizations.

Because most of what goes on inside a modern organization has little to do with truth.

*   *   *

Exercise 3: Looking at Control

This exercise will allow you to consider the ways in which your organization controls its workforce and compare those methods against your personal values.

1. Rank order the following control methods in terms of what extent your organization uses them to achieve order:
    —Policies and Procedures
    —Professionalism
    —Control through Vision
    —Planning
2. What other means not listed in this chapter does your organization employ to control the workforce?
3. To what degree do you think the controls are reasonable or unreasonable?
4. What is your organization's style of control—direct or indirect? How do you feel about it?
5. How do the controls imposed by the organization affect you? If they do not affect you, what groups are they designed to affect?

EVERYTHING BUT THE TRUTH

It should come as no surprise that in a culture that does not value truth, its organizations and institutions do not value it either.

Truth-telling is a rare commodity in any workplace. What you get instead are partial truths, old-fashioned stretchers and out and out lies. And I'm not just talking about the usual corporate doubletalk that we all know from press releases and investor conferences. People on every level of an organization seem to have a serious difficulty telling the whole truth and nothing but the truth. Managers lie to employees and employees lie right back to them, justifying dishonesty in the name of common sense. Work groups often isolate themselves from other groups within the organization to preserve various illusions. Truth avoidance is a force, a norm, a way of life that seemingly goes against everything parents teach their children, not to mention the good old tradition of truth, justice and the American way.

Truth avoidance occurs in nearly every activity of an organization. It starts in the recruiting and hiring processes and continues right through new employee orientation. It builds strength in weekly meetings and manager-employee confrontations. It is elevated to an art form with the technique of positioning, or what the world of television calls "spin doctoring." The avoidance of truth even follows one to the end of the employment road, whether that end is initiated by a layoff or by politics or by cause. Along with the control fetish, the avoidance of truth consumes more human energy than any other single activity inside an organization.

Of course, there are many good, sound, logical, practical and profitable reasons why truth rarely surfaces in corporate life. But before we get into the self-justification portion of the chapter, let's explore the phenomenon a little further.

Openness and Honesty

Because we wish to avoid getting too metaphysical regarding truth, we will avoid defining it in absolute terms and simply examine two practical measurements of truth: openness and honesty.

Openness involves the willingness and ability to share information with another. Honesty involves the accuracy of the information shared.

In most organizations, openness is not encouraged. The legitimate business need to avoid sharing trade secrets and other proprietary information with outsiders leads to a defensive paranoia that afflicts every corporation to some degree. Most operate under the philosophy that loose lips sink ships and you never know whom you can trust. The employee you trust today could be working for your competitor tomorrow, so sound business reasoning tells you to be careful as to what information you choose to share with whom.

There are two problems with this stance. The first is that establishing an atmosphere of distrust negatively affects both sides of the relationship. It's really a simple matter of you don't tell me, I don't tell you. The second is that because in most organizations, information equals power, the definitions of "proprietary" and "secret" are quite broad. Beyond a few generalities, privately held companies rarely share their financial situation with their employees. Executives often work out plans for expansion, layoffs, acquisitions and reorganizations in virtual isolation, favoring a few lucky people with tidbits that make the recipient feel important and secures their loyalty to the executive. In many ways, modern organizations are not much different from their medieval counterparts in the selective use of information to solidify and enhance power.

When we move on to the dimension of honesty, we also have to give organizations a less than passing grade. Boldface lies are not as common as what we call "positioning," the art of putting a positive spin on negative information. We see this in the statements that accompany financial reports, we see it in organizational announcements, and we see it when a company lays off people and reorganizes its staff. Some managers believe that positioning means sharing as little information as possible in order to preserve the option of denying potential misinterpretations.—However we position it, it must be stated that the failure to engage in open and honest communication starts at the top and therefore sets the tone for the entire organization. When information is power and executives encourage such a view by restricting the information flow, it encourages everyone else in the organization to do the same. People in survival situations—which is what we believe working for a living is all about—will first learn what it takes to survive before they begin thinking about other needs. Many people learn early in their working lives that to play the game, one must adopt a strategy towards co-workers and superiors that involves the manipulation of information to its best advantage.

Let's take a look at how this manifests itself in daily operations.

The Hiring Process

It is an astonishing fact that entering a long-term relationship with one's employer involves fundamental dishonesty on both sides. It is extremely difficult to make intelligent choices when all you have to work with are surrealist pictures. However, most recruiters choose to work in the style of Salvador Dali nonetheless.

Having been on both sides of the recruiting battlefield, I have to admit that I have engaged in truth avoidance on several occasions. Let me give you an example.

Once I was hiring a manager for a key position reporting to a vice-president. One of the candidates asked me what kind of guy this vice-president would be to work for.

What I said was, "Bill? Well, he's tough, but very achievement-oriented. Extremely focused. Defines the goals and goes after the results. He's got years of experience in the field and is totally committed to the company."

For those of you unfamiliar with organizational surrealism, I will translate:

"He's tough but very achievement-oriented." He's a major league asshole who blasts people in meetings and dresses them down in public. He cares more about the bottom line because of his expected bonus than he does about people or long-term goals.

"Extremely focused." He's a psychological cripple capable of only one thing in life, which is doing his job. He's obsessive like the character in Sherwood Anderson's "The Egg" but his egg hasn't broken yet. Doesn't have a life.

"Defines the goals and goes after the results." Definitely old-school management who sticks to conventional wisdom like management-by-objectives. Probably learned everything he thinks he needed to know years ago from another crusty old fart, no doubt a crusty male old fart.

"He's got years of experience in the field." As dogmatic as the Pope. Follows conventional wisdom even down the road to disaster.

"...and is totally committed to the company." Couldn't get a job elsewhere if his life depended on it.

Perceptive readers will note that not once did I tell an out-and-out lie. I didn't even stretch the truth; in fact, everything I said about the asshole was true. The real meaning of the message was more in what I did not say. This is a good example of the art of positioning, which reaches its creative heights in the areas of financial reporting and organizational announcements.

But back to our interview.

Now let's look at the person on the other side of the hiring desk: the candidate. You know, now that I think of it, I don't think the candidate was telling me the truth either.

Duh.

Everyone who has ever looked for a job knows that it's suicide to tell the truth when you're trying to get one. I can't think of a single employment interviewing book on the market that tells the prospective job hunter to tell the truth and demand the truth from the other side. All the advice is about how to get the job you want.

This is irresponsible advice, somewhat akin to taking your alcoholic friends to the local watering hole for a little socialization. Americans are programmed to want to *get*, even if they're not sure they even want what's gettable. If the media or influential friends have defined something as desirable, that's all that matters. If there is something out there to *get*, an American will go to great lengths to get it, no matter what it is. Our cultural history is littered with pet rocks.

This means that every candidate who goes into a job interview is out to get something, in this case, a job. That may seem obvious, but let's look at what they're not trying to achieve. They're not trying to give the company an honest picture of themselves and their experience. They're not being honest with themselves about their limitations but trying to "position" those limitations so that they can get. "Turn a weakness into a strength," the experts tell them.

So our typical American goes to the interview dressed in his or her Sunday best, spouting achievements, extolling virtues and otherwise selling the prospective employer on the proposition that a more perfect match for their needs does not exist in the known universe. The mistake made at the previous employer that cost the company a million bucks or a week's worth of production is selectively forgotten. Also avoided is that the real reason for pursuing this opportunity is because he or she is in serious debt and working at a company with a wage freeze, or that the motivation for going into management has something to do with a psychological need to show mom that he or she is a worthwhile human being.

No, instead, we get something like this:

Interviewer: You've told me about your greatest strength (not that I believe it for a minute but I really need to fill this job and you've just given me good justification for the documentation so I can cover my ass if you don't cut it). Now tell me about your greatest weakness (not that you'll tell me the truth but it's on the interview form and I have to ask the same questions over and over again to meet EEOC requirements).

Candidate: (Yeah, I remember this one from the book. Gosh, it's just like taking a final, isn't it?) Well, Kathy, I've got to tell you that I have a real strong ability to turn weaknesses into strengths and if there's one thing that I've learned in my career it's that you've always got to keep learning, keep improving to stay on top. In today's competitive environment, you've really got to stay one step ahead, which is why I'm going back to school to complete my Master's degree (well, I did send away for the catalog). I can tell you that people have told me that my greatest weakness is that I work too hard and care too much, but I don't know if that's true as much as it is true that I put everything I've got into making sure I'm doing the best possible job. (have I covered everything? gosh, this *is* just like a final!) But to answer your question directly (she'll like this; especially with a little self-deprecating laughter to reveal my underlying self-confidence), I've always had a hard time with algebra (which has nothing whatsoever to do with this job but you don't want to come across like you think you're perfect, do you?)

Of course, the candidate knows that the company isn't going to bother to check references because the company is fully aware that they won't get anything approaching useful information from previous employers. This is due to the legal paranoia pervading our society that limits safe information to job titles and dates of employment. You can pretty much say anything you want in an interview and regardless of how skilled the recruiter is, you can get away with saying almost anything to justify the premise that you are in fact an exceptionally swell human being.

Organizations have wised up to the fact that candidates are trying to screw them and have implemented extensive hiring procedures involving multiple interviews, testing and background checks. I know of one company (one of the so-called "best managed companies") that goes back seven years in their background checks and will fire you if you happened to leave your driver's license at home one day and were unlucky enough to get pulled over for a broken signal light. Others are using the "temp-to-perm" process, requiring job seekers to work without benefits for a few months so they can see how things work out (as if a desperate person motivated by getting couldn't toe the line for ninety days). They're not going to let you bastards get away with it, for Christ's sake!

Of course, the note of suspicion is clearly absent from the siren song of the hiring interview. All you hear from the hiring manager is sweetness and light about the great benefits package, the ideal working conditions and the opportunity, always the opportunity. They do their best to sell the position, partially because they need the help, and partially because the manager probably hasn't seen her kids in three months.

Tip: when you hear a prospective employer stress the "great opportunity to make a difference," terminate the interview. It means that the company is in a shambles and they want you to work twenty hours a day in a futile attempt to keep the dam from bursting. You will no longer have a life if you take this job.

So—you're looking for a job. The company hiring you knows you've inflated your resume and turned your mistakes into positive learning experiences. You know the company is giving you a load of horsefeathers when they start talking about opportunity and "the great people at Acme Enterprises." Both sides are avoiding the truth as if it were the most shameful disease known to humanity.

What a way to start off a relationship. Gosh, if we started our romantic relationships this way, our divorce rate in this society would be well over fifty percent.

Oops.

Life with the Boss

Now that you're hired, your most important relationship is the one you have with your boss. This is never an easy relationship, largely because its success depends on your ability to know how far to go with open and honest communication.

We have a "workplace advice columnist" in our local paper who dispenses suggestions to people who write to her about problems they're having on the job, legal rights and other related questions. In one of her first columns, a questioner told her how he had a job interview scheduled with another employer and wondered if he should "do the right thing" and tell the boss what was going on. I don't remember the exact response she gave but I do remember the gist of it.

"Are you nuts?"

I've often told managers in my training classes that the key to successful company-wide employee relations is successful manager-employee relationships. That these relationships are rarely successful has as much to do with truth avoidance as it has to do with the interpersonal shortcomings that afflict many a supervisor.

In general, you do have to be nuts to tell your boss the truth. There are several reasons for this:

Egos Run Wild: It is certainly unwise to tell a boss with a Napoleonic complex that their idea is silly, that their opinion is questionable or that their tie doesn't match any known possibility within the visible color spectrum. An egomaniac will resent you forever, making life unnecessarily difficult for you.

Loyalty Oaths: Many managers act as if an employee engaging in the free labor market is committing an act of treason (of course, it's okay if they do it themselves). Happening to mention to your boss that a headhunter gave you a call or that you've heard that Acme Enterprises is hiring can bring on all sorts of paranoid questions about your intentions. In some corporations, even looking for another job inside the company can get you blacklisted.

Help Me Cover My Ass: Bosses rarely want to know about mistakes that will make them look bad. What they want to know is how you have managed to cover up the mistake and then deflected blame away from the boss to a managerial rival in another department. What they'll tell you is "don't come to me with problems, come to me with solutions!"

Even good leaders can fall prey to these weaknesses from time to time, particularly if they are good people hopelessly entwined by personal financial obligations in an extremely political organization. A leader has to have some sense of ego, some level of belief in him or herself, to ever think of taking a leadership position in the first place. Leaders know that they have to accept responsibility for all the mistakes made in their organization and that there are plenty of people lurking around just waiting for the opportunity to point an accusing finger at their incompetence. This encourages the fervent wish that nothing go wrong and if it does, that it be "positionable." Pressure from above or bad timing can make anyone leaving them seem like a personal affront, largely because they know they're the ones who are going to have to do the work if somebody leaves (unless they have a status hang-up, in which case the work won't get done at all).

Organizational Announcements

As you become more involved in the life of the organization, from time to time you will receive communication in the form of what is called an organizational announcement. These usually deal with personnel matters, since people inside organizations are just as obsessed with people-watching as they are when they go home and watch *Entertainment Tonight* and read *People* magazine. Organizations also use announcements to communicate company results and new developments. Some organizations have extensive electronic communications systems utilizing E-mail, closed-circuit television and sundry other devices to get the word out to their employees.

If you guessed that I'm going to tell you that most of what goes out in the form of organizational announcements is bullshit, you are one perceptive reader.

Take the typical announcement that an executive is leaving the organization. Isn't it always to "pursue other career opportunities"? This, of course, is often a euphemism for "we fired the incompetent boob." You cannot call the person an incompetent boob, however, for not only would this be bad form but would also cause packs of attorneys to descend upon the company like vultures smacking their lips over fresh carrion.

In his wonderful book *Maverick*, Brazilian business leader Ricardo Semler describes his company's approach to organizational announcements:

> At Semco we rarely fire anyone for cause, but when we do, we don't put a notice up on the bulletin board announcing, "Mr. Pilfer has decided to resign, regrettably, for reasons of health. If an employee has breached our confidence, we say so. If he has left for a better job, we say that, too, wish him well, and sometimes express the hope that he will one day return.
>
> We always try to speak the truth and nothing but the truth. And on those rare occasions when the truth, for some special reason, cannot be told, we say nothing. We believe it is essential that all company communications, especially those intended for the workers or the public, be absolutely honest.

Imagine that approach in any American corporation! With the unvarnished truth, employees might be able to make intelligent choices as to whether or not they want to spend the majority of their waking hours at a particular workplace. Investors might be able to make intelligent choices about whether or not to invest their money in a company. Although I personally deplore the lawsuit mania pervading this country, one has to admit that in many cases companies fall into a trap of their own devising. People get infuriated when they feel they are being jerked around, and while I have known of instances where companies have been sued because they told the truth to an employee who was psychologically incapable of handling it, most complaints are grounded in the bullshit that organizations feel obligated to produce in a weak attempt to defend themselves from complaints.

But there is another side to the story.

Do Whatever You Like to Me, But Don't Tell Me the Truth

People avoid the truth because they need to preserve various illusions. Many an employee who cheats the company out of time and occasional office supplies will become quite indignant if their integrity is questioned. Investors don't want the company into which they've just poured in a chunk of their life savings to make any statements that can adversely affect the stock price. Neither employees nor investors are very strong on the ability to accept responsibility for their choices. It's always someone else's fault: the boss is an asshole, the company lied to me, they never told me it would be this way.

The primary illusion Americans need to have is that they are "successful," or more accurately, that family, friends and other important luminaries believe they're "doing well." Consequently, a great portion of one's self-esteem is tied to one's occupation. Upon meeting someone for the first time, the opening question is invariably, "What do you do?" Occupation is a fundamental part of our identity within society. Hence the reason so many people become depressed when they lose their jobs, even when the loss is through no fault of their own and even though they know that organizational validation is fairly meaningless, given the number of incompetents who populate them. We lose not only our incomes but also our identities.

Since our self-image is so thoroughly tied to our jobs, it also follows that one is not going to be extremely open to hearing any kind of adverse feedback about job performance, even if such feedback is given in the most helpful manner possible. The more insecure the person, the more violent the reaction. Often a person will avoid any attempt at self-reflection by blaming the person guilty of truth-telling.

Although those of you who believe in the media babble about lean and mean companies may still not believe it, let me repeat what I said in the previous chapter: people are very rarely fired for performance in any organization. It isn't only because the HR people, watching the company's legal behind, make the manager go through an extensive three or four step process through which enough documentation is created to fill a row of filing cabinets. It is because it is very difficult to tell another human being that they are failing. To tell an American he or she is a failure is akin to shooting them in the heart. You are attacking their very essence, their reason for existence, their entire concept of self-worth. In telling an employee they aren't cutting it, you are risking legal problems, threats and in some cases, the possibility of violence.

I remember listening to a psychologist on the radio around the time of the 101 California tragedy. He said that a common trait linking perpetrators of workplace violence was their inability to accept responsibility. I would venture that the same could be said for people who file lawsuits, many of which represent the use of a legally sanctioned form of extortion. Both are weapons to use against the enemy who has punctured the mask.

So what motivation is there for a manager to tell an employee the truth? Beyond the slim possibility that the feedback might help the employee become more effective in the future, there isn't any. Managers do not feel the need to intervene in an employee's life simply because that employee's parents didn't do a very good job of instilling any responsibility in them. It's much safer for a manager to work around the problem by making up reasons to add headcount, reassigning work to others or just doing the work oneself.

And the truth continues to suffer.

The Hygiene Factor

There are also certain employee relations situations that are just plain awkward, even if it weren't for the veneer of professional conduct that adds a level of unnecessary formality to any organization.

Take, for example, the employee with a hygiene problem.

What happens is the employee begins emitting an odor. This odor spreads to the nostrils of co-workers and they are offended by it. However, the co-workers never feel it is their responsibility to say anything about it, so they complain to the manager. The manager feels a sinking feeling in his or her stomach because they think they're responsible for dealing with this problem and they do not have the slightest idea how to go about it.

So they go to Human Resources for assistance. HR doesn't want to deal with it any more than the manager does, so a tug of war takes place. "He's your employee," says HR. "But I thought HR was here to help me with difficult situations," says the manager. "I can help you think things through, I can do a role play, I can even be there with you but you're going to have to face him." Grumble, grumble.

A manager once called me for help on how to deal with a hygiene problem. We worked through some possible approaches for about an hour or so, then I told her to keep in touch. I found out later that what she did was give the employee in question a promotion so she could physically move him to another part of the building where he wouldn't be within sensor range of other people.

It didn't do any good to argue with the manager that she would be doing this employee a favor by pointing out the problem. Perhaps the employee was simply unaware of it. Perhaps the employee's love life was also being affected and he couldn't figure out why. In some cases, a hygiene problem results from a medical condition; in others, it reveals a cultural prejudice on the part of finicky, deodorant-worshipping Americans.

The main point is that it was a potentially embarrassing situation that lent itself perfectly to the truth avoidance mechanisms available to an organization. Now we had a happy if ignorant employee whose ego had been inflated by a promotion. The next poor manager who comes in and finds that the employee is not cutting it will find it virtually impossible to terminate him. Both the manager and the employee became part the organizational conspiracy against truth, to the detriment of all concerned.

The Fear Factor

Beyond the awkward situations of communicating adverse information regarding performance and personal habits, there is a more serious factor preventing people from telling the truth in the workplace.

This is the fear of losing one's job.

The motivation to get, get, get leads Americans to make all sorts of financial arrangements from car payments to mortgages to credit card bills. Therefore, the possibility of losing one's source of income becomes a very scary prospect. The argument is basically, "Why should I stick my neck out? It's not worth it. Just shut up, do your job and leave well enough alone."

This fear exists on every level of an organization. Executives make the same kind of financial commitments that less-compensated members of the organization make, but on a grander scale. Furthermore, they have more status points to lose by speaking out. I believe that the higher you go in an organization, the greater the level of fear of telling the truth. You have much more to lose when you are on top.

By the way, this explains most of the brownnosing that goes on inside a corporation, for ass-kissing occurs primarily in the management and executive ranks. It also explains why so many vice-presidents are abusive to their subordinates. After a tough, all-day session of swallowing their true thoughts and feelings so as to avoid pissing off the boss, they have to take it out on someone.

Most of the fear of speaking out is based on rumor. People "have heard" that so-and-so was forced out because they didn't toe the line or because they dared disagree with their boss. When you try to argue that there is nothing in the company's documentation to support the belief that people get fired for speaking out, the savvy organizational member will pity you for your naiveté. "They have ways of getting you," they'll say knowingly.

Well, the truth is "they" sometimes do. I've known executives go through extensive and complex reorganizations to get rid of one person who was a pain in the ass. I've seen layoffs structured to exploit every loophole of company policy to ensure that the troublemakers get the ax.

The problem is not that this sometimes happens. The problem is the effect of fear on the level of truth within an organization.

I demonstrate this dilemma in some of my training programs through the use of a case study called "Beverly, Crushed." Here's the story:

It was about three months ago that the idea to simplify some of her department's procedures first popped into Beverly's head. At first she dismissed it as silly, but as time went on and she continued to encounter the same problems over and over, she became more and more convinced that her idea had merit. The idea became so powerful that finally she felt she simply had to get it on paper to see if it really was feasible. Beverly worked through an entire weekend putting her thoughts in order and created a proposal she felt would streamline operations and improve efficiency.

On Monday, though, she decided to leave the proposal at home. She wanted to think it over before sharing it with anyone, just to make sure.

On Wednesday, she attended a meeting with her boss and several of her peers. One of the topics of the meeting was to discuss the very procedures Beverly wanted to change. She saw this as an opportunity to present at least a rough summary of her proposal and test the waters, so to speak.

When the topic came up, Beverly began by giving a brief overview of her proposal. About halfway through her spiel, her boss cut her off. "Yes, Beverly, you're exactly right! I was doing some thinking and I came up with this." The boss then distributed a summary of her own proposal to the group. Much to Beverly's dismay, the proposal would have made the work much more complicated. It wasn't anything like what Beverly had come up with.

The boss asked for opinions. Beverly listened as one by one each of her peers nodded agreement. "Okay, Bev, we haven't heard from you," said her boss, looking at her with expectation. Beverly straightened up and cleared her throat. "To be honest…" she began, but stopped herself when she felt the weight of all of those eyes on her. "Yes, to be honest, I think we can make it work." "Okay," said the boss, "let's do it." The meeting then adjourned and the boss left the room.

As she was packing up to go, one of her colleagues came up to her and said, "It looked like you wanted to say something." Beverly bit her lip. "No, not really," she said. Her colleague looked at her skeptically for a moment and then said knowingly, "It's probably just as well—you know how the boss doesn't like to be challenged in front of the group. After all, look what happened to Julian." Beverly wasn't quite sure what happened to Julian (all she knew was that he left the company a couple of months ago), but she understood what her colleague was trying to say.

Beverly left the meeting with two action items to help implement something she knew wasn't going to work. Even though she had serious doubts and thought that her boss was too far removed from reality to make an effective decision, she went ahead and implemented them anyway. Of course, the inevitable happened. People started complaining about how it was taking them almost twice as long to finish the job before the change was implemented. They came to her and told her that it just flat out wasn't going to work. "I knew it!" Beverly said to them. "Don't worry; I'll bring it up at next week's meeting."

Because the new procedures were not part of the agenda, Beverly waited until the end of the meeting for the five minutes the group allotted to cover anything not on the agenda. "I wanted to talk about the new procedures," she began. "Is there a problem?" her boss asked, gathering her papers and obviously getting ready to charge off to her next meeting. "Uh, no, well, people are having a little trouble with—" Her boss cut her off again. "Well, people are always resistant to change," the boss said. "Anything else?" There was silence and everyone went their separate ways.

That night, Beverly went home and tore up her proposal.

I have the class break up into small groups and ask them to go through the case study and answer some questions. The first set is designed to get participants to realize that Beverly was not forced into doing anything: she had choices every step of the way.

Q: Review Beverly's choices and identify what beliefs and/or feelings may have motivated each choice:
The decision not to put anything on paper when she first had the idea
The decision to leave her proposal at home so she could think it over some more
The decision to give a rough summary of her idea at the first meeting
The decision not to disagree with the proposal put forward by her boss
The choice not to share her idea with her colleague
The decision to voice her true opinions to the people who worked for her when they came to complain about the new proposal
The decision not to assert herself at the second meeting but to let the explanation of "resistance to change" stand unchallenged

The rest of the questions focus on what Beverly could have done differently, what she should do now, what the boss could have done differently and the like.

At this point in the case study, groups have various opinions of Beverly. Younger people and sales types label her a "wimp". The general audience feels sorry for Beverly but they agree that she isn't very effective and probably should look for a new job.

It is at this point that I give them the clincher. I ask them to reconvene in their groups and ponder the following question:

"It just so happens that Beverly is a single parent and the sole support of two small children. How does this impact your understanding of Beverly's course of action in this scenario?"

The room explodes in controversy. "It doesn't make any difference!" some people shout. "Hey, would you challenge the boss if you were in that situation?" respond the others. "You've got to take risks in life!" the wimp-callers shoot back. "Take a risk with the lives of two little kids?" respond the more sympathetic.

There is no traditional resolution to the case study. The point is to demonstrate that everyone who enters the workplace increases their level of vulnerability by taking on personal and financial obligations. Vulnerability affects risk-taking and decision-making because the greater the sense of vulnerability, the greater the fear of speaking out.

What we have to realize is that despite those obligations, there is always a deeper existential responsibility as captured in the phrase, "in the end, you have to live with yourself." Every person who enters an organization at one time or another is faced with this ethical dilemma and most simply cave in, kiss some more ass and buy a new car. When you confront them on it, they point out the impossibility of changing anything because of the boss, because of the policies, because of anything else that doesn't reflect their own lack of ability or courage.

When one is not true to oneself, it is difficult to be true to others. The fear of speaking out is a manifestation of the more fundamental untruth that pervades organizations as well as our society: people are generally not willing to be true to themselves.

The Bottom Line

The impact of norms of dishonesty and closed communication is fairly significant. Deming has remarked that a company cannot have quality without accurate information. Failing to encourage the truth can have dire consequences, for when mistakes are made, the information is positioned in such a way that the error becomes difficult to detect. You never really know what you're dealing with until it is too late to do anything about it—after the mistake has been discovered by the customer.

Furthermore, the need to keep a lid on the truth requires a lot of energy. It is old wisdom that it is easier to tell the truth because then you can keep your story straight. A vast quantity of human energy is wasted in the political in-fighting, positioning and game-playing that accompanies norms of non-truth.

Although leaders set the tone for their organizations and have the power to prevent people from engaging in open and honest communication, we cannot blame our leaders for the mess. We all participate in the conspiracy against truth. The failure to tell the truth is a problem in the larger society, encouraged by our need to play victim when it is to our advantage, by our constant desire to accumulate, by our willingness to live according to the expectations of others and by lacking confidence in our own abilities and power. The situation cannot change unless individual human beings decide to make a commitment to the truth, regardless of the risks.

Remember: the most important issue in organizational life is and will always be your own integrity.

*   *   *

Exercise 4: Looking at Truth

Although I should not have to tell you to be honest with yourself while completing an exercise on truth, it is necessary because of the endless human capacity for self-deception. For this exercise, you may want to share your answers with a colleague to get their feedback because it is very difficult to have an objective viewpoint on this topic.

1. To what extent does your organization practice open and honest communication? Give examples to support your opinion.

2. To what extent do you practice open and honest communication in the workplace? Review your relationships in the workplace and rank them high, medium or low on openness and honesty.

	Openness	*Honesty*
My Colleagues		
My Supervisor		
My Direct Reports		
Upper Management		
Customers		
Vendors		
Other:		

3. Look back to when you were hired. To what extent were you honest about your situation? To what extent was the company honest about the opportunity?

4. Read three to five recent organizational communications and give them a grade on the level of truth, with "A" being perfectly truthful and "F" being completely untruthful.

5. How many people like Beverly exist in your organization? To what extent do people avoid sharing ideas and opinions out of fear of the consequences?

THE CURIOUS NOTION OF LEADERSHIP

When you go to work, the organization will provide you with someone to oversee your work. This person is called a boss, a supervisor or a manager (although in less polite circles, stronger language has been used to describe these individuals).

Now you may think that after exposing the weaknesses of corporate entities in the matters of status, control and truth, the author intends to adhere to the path traveled by management theorists from Deming onwards and blame anywhere from 80 to 100% of the problem on management.

Nope.

Let me contend that regardless of how well we pay executives, administrators, football coaches and political leaders; regardless of the status, prestige and sometimes public attention we give them; and regardless of the aphrodisiac qualities we attribute to the pursuit and attainment of power; there is one fundamental truth that the theorists and authors of our best-selling management books have completely ignored.

Being a leader *sucks*.

The reason for this is our society has an exceedingly unrealistic perspective on leadership. We hold leaders accountable for everything that happens, from plummeting stock prices to natural disasters, even if the leader is powerless to do anything about it. If the economy goes south, we blame the President, even though the President has extremely limited powers under our Constitution and has even less of an impact on the short-term results of the American economy. We hold on to the myth, though, that there are magic leaders like Lee Iacocca and Colin Powell who have track records to show that one person can make a difference.

Were Iacocca and Powell effective leaders? Certainly. Did they do it all by themselves? Impossible. I repeat, all work in any organization is by nature a cooperative venture, and there is no way any leader can achieve any goal without the help and cooperation of those being led.

These unrealistic expectations of leadership also create a psychological dynamic where the leader's lap becomes the convenient dumping ground for any problems that may arise. Leaders become the primary focus for unhappy shareholders and unhappy employees, who place tremendous pressure on a single person to deliver often unrealistic results. Because we have a long history of trashing leaders, from Washington to Truman to the present occupant of the White House, it may be that one function of leaders is to give us a psychological release by becoming easily accessible objects for scorn and derision. Perhaps leaders exist primarily to enable us to escape responsibility for our problems. On the other hand, since we also glamorize our leaders and put them on pedestals, it could be argued that leaders serve as objects of our creative and destructive urges by representing both ideal possibility and unpleasant reality. Whatever the dynamic, the truth is that if you want to be a leader, be prepared to take some hits, for you will be abused as frequently as a quarterback behind a porous offensive line.

If you have strong psychological tendencies towards masochism or martyrdom, if you want to earn a big pile of money without ever having the time to enjoy it, if you want to attempt to balance impossible demands coming at you from up, down and outside your organization, and if your need to prove to your daddy that you are somebody matters more to you than your health and well-being, then by all means, be a leader.

After all, that's why they'll pay you the big bucks.

The Myth of the Man of Action

"Ah," you say, "but I have no psychological problems, I'm willing to do whatever it takes, I like a good challenge and my parents accept me for who I am. The reason I want to be a leader is I want to get things done!"

"Poor misguided soul," I respond.

Jennifer James is probably right in saying that the enduring myth of the cowboy, particularly the Lone Ranger, is the source of our mistaken beliefs about leadership. We seem to operate under the one-man theory of leadership (emphasis on the male gender) where we believe that one guy can get in there and clean up the goddamn mess we're in. Hence the attraction to Iacocca and Powell, and hence the counterargument given above that no leader can do it alone.

And often leaders can't do it at all.

I remember I was in the men's room one day when our new CEO came in to take care of personal business. While we were chatting amiably at the washstands, I noticed he was struggling with the soap dispensers, which had never worked properly in the five years I had been with that particular company. Finally he said, "There are two things I'm going to accomplish before they throw me out of here. The first is to make this place profitable again and the second is to fix these goddamn soap dispensers."

Sure enough, he started on his quest for excellence in sanitation shortly after our encounter. A couple of weeks later I saw the Facilities Manager installing new soap dispensers in the men's room. Sure enough, they didn't work any better than the old ones. What had happened is that unbeknownst to the CEO, the accounting folks had kicked back the original request for top-of-the-line soap dispensers due to budget limitations imposed by the CEO himself. The Facilities Manager had then purchased an off-brand that, like its predecessor, refused to produce any soap.

A couple of months later, the CEO confronted the Facilities Manager, who explained what happened. The CEO went to the accounting people and told them to waive the financial restrictions on this order of soap dispensers. He told the Facilities Manager to go for it, but by that time, the Facilities Department was engaged in a high-priority office move and the soap dispensers were forgotten. By the time the Facilities Manager finally got around to it, the price of the soap dispensers had gone up and the request was once again kicked back to him.

This went on for several more months, until, finally, the Facilities Manager had the Cadillac of Soap Dispensers in hand. He went on vacation for a few weeks and left the job to an underling, who was immediately swamped with urgent requests from everyone in the building and forgot about the soap dispensers. The Facilities Manager returned to find the dispensers still in their boxes and rushed over to the men's room closest to the CEO to install them. Sadly, the wall holding the soap dispensers had so many holes in it that it was difficult to find a place where the dispensers would stick. After much poking and drilling, he managed to get them on the wall. A few days later he received a phone call that half of his soap dispensers were now lying on the floor in puddles of pink goo. The CEO finally said the hell with it and moved on to other things. When I left the company three years later, the soap dispensers were still non-functional.

This is but a small example of the limitations on the power of a leader. Even with the support of the people around them, it is difficult for a leader to get anything done. There are hidden rules and procedures strewn across the organizational battlefield like landmines, waiting to explode even the best intentions. There are countless opportunities for miscommunication up, down and across the hierarchy. And as everybody knows, people have a way of pretending not to understand orders from above and either stall for time by pointing out apparently serious but exaggerated complications or by ignoring the original order altogether. They can always say that no one told them (adding, "and nobody ever tells me anything") or that they didn't hear it right or that they thought you meant something else. Much of what we identify as "resistance to change" is really the sport of screwing around with the boss.

This is one of the paradoxes of hierarchy. One reaches the top in pursuit of power and status to find that one has limited power and that status does not ensure obedience. Leaders in hierarchies have far more negative power than positive power. They can stop things from happening by denying expenditures and rejecting proposals but they have very little power to achieve goals that their subordinates either do not want to achieve or are not capable of achieving. They can make threats, they can pound tables, they can scream at the top of their lungs but unless leaders do what the people below them want done, very little will happen.

This is why leaders often play favorites, for there are always a few people in any organization currying favor from above who will do just about anything for the leader. Leaders find those people out and give them the dirty work, like announcing layoffs or pay cuts. They will give them "secret missions" to infiltrate the bureaucracy and get something done. In exchange for a little servility, these people get relative job security and the thrill of feeling they are more important than the others. The leader gets a few things accomplished and what is more important, builds a protective wall of toadies around him or her for added protection from the various potshots aimed in his or her direction.

Under Siege

Since leaders are under attack from all sides, whatever their position in the organization, it is natural that leaders would have a tendency to protect themselves. Leaders, I remind you, are human beings just like everyone else. They don't like rejection and they don't particularly care for abuse.

This need to protect oneself from the slings and arrows of outrageous employees, bosses and customers causes leaders to seek isolation. Leaders take refuge in several typical organizational cubbyholes designed in large part to increase their status by making them inaccessible but in small part to give them some time to escape the battle. Here are the primary activities leaders engage in to achieve solitude:

Meetings: One extremely successful method leaders use to escape day-to-day reality is to schedule meetings—lots of meetings. It may sound strange that one would seek out other human beings to escape human beings but the human beings in meetings are often fellow leaders also seeking relative tranquility. Since nothing is ever accomplished in meetings, one's serenity is rarely disturbed by having to think or act. Because meetings are so frequent and always run late, they also provide a convenient excuse for not having done one's job, as in "Boy, I could really get some work done if I didn't have to spend all day in meetings." Meetings become a very effective means of keeping unpleasant people at bay. "I'm in a meeting right now" is a convenient excuse used to dispose of unwelcome callers, and "she's in a meeting" is a handy phrase for the secretary to use to terminate the complaints of nasty customers wanting to take a bite out of the leader's hide.

It is important to remember that the further down you are in the hierarchy, the more meetings you will have to schedule to fill up your calendar. Executives have the option of the all-day meeting, which they use to great effect, raising their status by becoming completely inaccessible. For those lower in the organization, though, you have to allow some time between meetings to respond to the unreasonable demands foisted on you by executives working in isolation.

Stock Phrases: There are several canned phrases leaders use to gain time and distance from the maddening crowd. Some of the most popular delaying tactics are:

> *"Uh, let me get back to you on that."*
> *"We're working on that."*
> *"Let's do lunch some time."*
> *"Come to me with solutions, not problems."*
> *"I'm late for a meeting."*
> *"Send me a proposal."*

Technology has given us new stock phrases by providing leaders with suitable reasons for not getting back to a person, as in "no, I didn't get that voice mail," or "sorry, our system is down again." Some leaders have taken the idea one step further by not even bothering with the etiquette of the stock phrase. They just ignore the message, memo or request and go about their business. If ignoring requests results in a customer or employee going over their heads to their superior, the oblivious leader can then use the "we're working on that" approach or blame either the system or a poor schmuck in another department for the miscommunication.

Tablets: Another effective method of keeping one's distance from the riffraff is to communicate in memo form (in those rare instances where the leader feels they absolutely have to communicate something). I call these tablets because they appear about as frequently as Moses coming down from the mountain.

Successful tablet communication consists of two steps. The first is to write a memo that says as little as possible and positions bad news as something that is necessary for the continuing survival of the company. For example, here is the opening paragraph of a typical tablet I picked up from a Fortune 500 company:

> As Acme Enterprises as grown into a dynamic organization, we have continued to improve our processes and systems to keep pace with rapid expansion and with the competitive world in which we live. Today we are announcing significant improvements to our administrative processes that will enhance our ability to serve our customers in the most cost-effective manner possible.

Six paragraphs later, the ax falls on about one hundred employees.

Note the careful and artistic use of business cliché in the typical tablet: "the competitive world in which we live" and "to enhance our ability to serve our customers" and "the most cost-effective manner possible." This is very safe inarguable language that creates the impression of conscientious, thoughtful leaders. Usually, however, the truth is they have just discovered a major screw-up that is going to compromise the annual bonus and they have to scurry around to find something to cut.

Oh, yes. The second element of a successful tablet is: never make yourself available to answer questions. Distribute the memo through the mail system or have a subordinate make the announcement for you. The latter approach has the advantage of automatic denial, for if you have followed proper status maintenance techniques, the subordinate will know nothing and therefore can use the ultra-safe stock phrases noted above to maintain distance. If you have a secretary, have him or her make the calls to find out how things are going.

The effect of all this isolation is bad decision-making that is often out of touch with how the rest of the organization perceives reality. Isolation is a key symptom of GroupThink, that false consensus that results in often disastrous decisions. In spite of all the hype about cross-functional teams, most companies still work departmentally, which means their staff meetings are closed to people from other departments. This failure to consider outside views or different perspectives can make for a sort of bunker mentality, especially if the group is under pressure (and what group isn't?). Reality becomes whatever the group in its isolation wants it to be, and stuck on their dogma, they produce decisions and actions that frequently seem absurd to the rest of the organization.

So, in addition to incredible pressure and a gradually dawning awareness of one's impotence, the scorn heaped upon a leader eventually leads to isolation and utter ineffectiveness.

Remember that the next time someone offers you an opportunity to move into management.

Three Versions of Leaders

Okay, I will admit that leadership is not all tar and feathers. It can be a satisfying experience for those leaders who have the skill, courage and confidence to lead a group or organization to solid achievement. If you're interested in helping people grow and you get to watch them develop into responsible people who find out that they are far more capable than they thought, the experience can be emotionally gratifying. Leadership positions give people the opportunity to realize their vision by giving them an invitation to exercise power in the name of progress. While you can have an impact on an organization from a non-management role, being in a position of authority gives you some credibility at the start; the "honeymoon" period for new leaders has been well documented (although it seems to be growing shorter).

If leadership appeals to you, there are also several excellent books on the subject to guide you towards the development of a coherent approach to leadership. Covey's *Principle-Centered Leadership* is a fine book, as is the Kouzes-Posner classic *The Leadership Challenge*. Both emphasize the importance of self-reflection as a prerequisite for building trust between you and your constituents. Both books are value-oriented in that they clearly establish the ethical foundations of leadership: trustworthiness, honesty, competence and the acceptance of responsibility.

Of course, there are many unethical, untrustworthy, irresponsible leaders who achieved their positions through a single-minded focus on personal success and through the ability to use power to crush other people on their way to the top. The ethic of toughness that re-emerged in the 1980's as America went paranoid about foreign competition created a cadre of tough, unsympathetic leaders who are intelligent enough to pay lip service to new leadership theory but run their organizations in a more Machiavellian manner. Still, these leaders do not constitute the majority, for my experience tells me that about half of the people in leadership positions are decent, well-meaning people trying to do their best under often intense pressure and without much thought as to their professional development. I estimate that the unethical tough guys and gals make up about ten percent of the leadership population. Unfortunately, many of them are in the higher levels of the organization where they do inflict great damage with their short-term, success-driven personalities.

And the other forty percent? These are folks that don't have a clue what's going on around them. They got into leadership for all the wrong reasons: because it was a rare promotional opportunity, because they wanted to impress people, because they wanted more money, because their ego needed a boost, because they happened to be the only person around willing to take the job. These leaders infuriate people with their incompetence and have an annoying tendency to get in the way of progress by interfering in matters about which they know nothing but feel that because they are leaders they should be involved. Generally incapable of making a decision or taking a stand, they are among the most unpopular leaders on the planet. People prefer known quantities in their leaders, and even the most extreme fascist is sometimes preferable to a jellyfish because at least you know what you're getting.

Choosing a Leader

What sort of leader one admires depends largely on one's set of values. There are people who prefer highly directive leaders who tell them exactly what to do. There are others who would prefer it if the leader would take a permanent vacation in a place with no access to any form of telecommunications. Some like leaders who are risk-takers; others prefer the more conservative types who keep a steady hand on the wheel. Since a leader is often the embodiment of one's personal aspirations, it would make sense that we would admire those qualities that we either have or wish we had ourselves.

The leaders I have admired are people who are willing to admit that they don't know something, not afraid to admit a mistake when they make one (as long as they don't make too many), care about the people around them but are able to put up a fight when organizational norms demand it, and above all, keep going in the face of numerous setbacks and unforeseen obstacles. This is because I personally value learning (and you can't learn if you can't admit you don't know everything), growth (the entire purpose of making mistakes), compassion (and there are times I wish I had more of that quality) and perseverance (because there have been too many times when I've given up too easily). You may have a different set of desired leadership qualities, such as intelligence or a sense of humor or the ability to inspire confidence. The point is that we judge our leaders based upon our own personal standards of what we think a leader should be and then compare a leader's actions—always the actions, never the words—to those personal standards. This is important for two reasons: one, those expectations we place on leaders make it difficult for them to be human (after all, no one can live up to the ideal); and two, those projected values are often rendered irrelevant because leaders are not chosen according to our own set of values.

Or any other set of values.

Most leaders are not chosen based upon their inherent qualities, their ability to inspire others or that they are decent human beings. Most leaders are chosen out of convenience. This means that leaders are selected by whatever process involves the least amount of hassle to the person making the selection. The existence of "the old boys' network" owes itself to this laziness, for it is always easier to pick someone you know and with whom you feel comfortable than it is to have to go through the hassle of interviewing a bunch of strangers. Sometimes leadership positions are automatically given to whoever has the most tenure in the work group, regardless of their personal qualities or leadership skills. Sometimes leadership positions are given to whoever's left after a reorganization or to the dummy who happened to be the only person who applied for the job.

Now this process (if one can call it that) may strike some of you as being inherently unfair. It may strike others as another confirmation of the Peter Principle. The unfairness is real; trying to prove it or do anything about it is problematic. Any Human Resources professional or any halfway-competent lawyer can produce a line of argument justifying a contested promotion that would make an EEOC auditor's head spin. Furthermore, as one lawyer pointed out to me, "while there may be laws preventing discrimination, there are no laws to stop management from making stupid decisions." The slowness and hassle of the EEO complaint process deters many people; others turn away from filing a complaint because they know that doing so attaches a stigma to one's career aspirations. The regulations preventing retaliation are unenforceable for the most part; the sort of retaliation organizations engage in is of the subtle, behind-the-back variety that results in easy denial.

The Real Leadership Challenge

The crisis our world faces in relation to leadership goes deeper than how to select leaders and then give them the skills they need to do the job. Kouzes and Posner are entirely right by saying that leadership is a set of skills that can be learned. While there are many leaders in government, corporate America and the non-profit sector who could use some serious skill-building, the problem has little to do with training and development.

The problem now is that hardly anybody in their right mind would want to be a leader.

Colin Powell dropped out of presidential consideration for some very good reasons. Why put yourself and your loved ones through an essentially humiliating process in which their privacy and yours will be repeatedly violated by the media? Why bother to make speeches on the pressing issues of our times when your thoughts will be reduced to sound bytes and you will certainly be quoted out of context? And why on earth would anyone with any sense agree to be a leader of an organization, the United States Government, whose employees are generally despised and whose decision-making processes are governed by backroom deals and special interest investment? It is not a macho issue of whether or not someone has enough staying power to stand the heat. The current set of variables in political life make it virtually impossible to get anything done, and leaders are essentially people who feel the need to get things done.

On a smaller scale, but no less painful to a human being, is the reality facing the typical manager in a corporation. Where is the motivation to confront an unproductive employee when he or she is likely to seek revenge in the form of a lawsuit, or even worse, by violence? It is much easier to either live with an employee or manipulate the system to have the non-contributor transferred to another department. When leaders are trying to lead people who have a limited concept of personal responsibility, the result is that leaders will inevitably take the blame for anything that goes awry, even an employee's own non-performance. Add to this the fact that people are more likely to seek responsibility in the person in authority (angry customers want to speak to the manager, not some customer service rep) and you have a no-win situation where the inability to act simply adds to the incredible stress many managers experience.

I know this may be hard for many readers to consider, but even the typical CEO of a large corporation is a human being. He (emphasis again on the male gender) may be an extremely overpaid human being and he may even be a paranoid, domineering, manipulative jerk. No matter how effectively he isolates himself behind the trappings of privilege and the distance of high status, he cannot escape the demands of greedy shareholders who want a quick bounce in the stock price, the incredibly rapid speed of technological change and its impact on the organization and the frustration of the people under him who are confused by the rapidity of change and are looking to the leader for answers. All the responsibility is placed in his lap, and while there may be a golden parachute waiting to cover his financial needs, no termination package can compensate for the humiliation of failure.

When the ax falls, there are many who will shout from the sidelines, "He deserved it, the overpaid son-of-a-bitch." This reflects another aspect of our culture manifested in organizational life, which is the absence of the concept of forgiveness. Jerry Harvey has written about this subject quite poignantly; however, little has changed since the publication of "The Asoh Defense" over twenty years ago. It isn't satisfying enough to watch someone fail; we have to rub their noses in it. We also have broadened our definition of failure to include accusation and speculation, so that if we hear that someone is potentially a crook or a sexist or an idiot, they are branded with that label forever and even if they make some kind of comeback, the suspicion never goes away. The concept of rehabilitation is a fading dream; we want to fry the criminals and hang the failures with full media coverage.

Our current philosophy of leadership involves nothing more than what Jung called "projection of the shadow." Leaders are the objects onto whom we project our sense of failure, our fears, our own human weaknesses. We punish leaders because we cannot accept our own failings. We transfer all responsibility to the leader and justify it by pointing to the money they earn or the status they hold. For some reason, we feel that if someone has more money or more power, they are open targets for dehumanization.

Yes, there are bad leaders. And yes, there are leaders throughout history who have perpetrated horrible and dehumanizing acts far more grievous than our petty attacks. This still does not justify the avoidance of our responsibility in the matter. Leaders only lead with the consent of their followers; as we have demonstrated, leaders can accomplish nothing without the help and cooperation of other people. Our leaders are not the problem—we are. And until we redefine our notions of leadership by abolishing the one-person myth and replacing it with a concept of shared responsibility, the problem will not go away.

The concept of shared leadership is a radical idea for Americans, as dozens of ex-baseball managers will tell you. When things go wrong, we fire the boss. Sometimes that makes a difference, but even the most developed leaders will tell you that they do not experience success one hundred percent of the time; even Lincoln was capable of making bad decisions; and that sometimes our most effective leaders were people who knew that it was best to do nothing in the circumstances presented to them. Perhaps if we started simply, with honest acceptance of our responsibility in the workplace, we could make leadership something desirable again.

*   *   *

Exercise 5: Looking at Leadership

Now it is time to look at how your organization exercises or fails to exercise leadership. Along the way we will take a look at your own leadership ambitions.

1. What does it take to move into a leadership position in your organization? Check all that apply:
    —Talent and ability
    —Willingness to take risks
    —Clear sense of vision
    —Ability to coach and motivate others
    —Good people skills
    —Integrity
    —Operational knowledge
    —It's who you know
    —The right gender, race, age, etc.

2. Now go back through the list and underline any of the dimensions that do not have an impact on the selection of leaders in your organization.

3. To what extent are your leaders accessible? If inaccessible, what are some of the reasons for it?

4. Describe your expectations of a leader.

5. Look at your expectations of a leader and evaluate how well you would live up to them if you were a leader in your organization (see note about being honest with yourself).

6. All things considered, does the possibility of a leadership position appeal to you? If not, why not? If so, under what circumstances and conditions?

To Choose or Not to Choose

So far we have talked about how most corporations of any size are problematic, to say the least. They are arenas where people compete for status as if they never left the schoolyard or the cave. They build systems of control around the paranoid tendencies of their leaders, their lawyers and their lightweights. Corporations are filled with people who find themselves lied to with amazing consistency and consequently learn to avoid the truth themselves. Finally, the corporate world reflects the larger culture in its severely limited notions of leadership and power.

We have demonstrated that there are advantages in such an environment, advantages that include relative stability and the opportunity for collaboration. For those who love to compete with their fellow human beings, corporate life offers many opportunities both within the company and outside in the marketplace. Still, the overall picture is not particularly attractive and it is less attractive when we understand that working for a corporation is the default choice of American life. To an outside observer, the situation must appear absurd. Why would an allegedly free people choose to work in such unpleasant environments? Since asking the people who take these jobs would only result in answers dripping with defensiveness, self-justification and a desire to avoid the truth at all costs, a survey of the working population would probably be a waste of time. Experience tells me that the answers are there, though, particularly if we look at the people who are on the verge of making a career decision.

Choosing Not to Choose

Recently I had the opportunity to teach a class in leadership at one of the local universities. The students were primarily seniors in their early twenties or graduates beginning their post-graduate work. A few were older people who had returned to school after disillusionment with their original choice. As part of the class introductions, I asked each person to tell me why they had chosen their particular field. The answers I received fell into four categories.

There were those who were clear about how they wanted to affect the world. For example, "I see how the arts can make a difference in instigating social change and I want to be involved in that."

There were some who weren't sure at all why they had chosen a particular field. They weren't sure for one of two reasons. The first was they had gone into it because it was what their parents had expected them to do. An equally common reason was that they had entered the field, found out they didn't care for it, but couldn't figure out how to back out gracefully, particularly after investing so much time working for the degree.

Some had chosen the field solely because of the job opportunities associated with it. "Software engineers are in great demand in the job market and I wanted to get in on that."

Finally, all the people who were returning to college were searching for something, even though they weren't exactly sure what that something was. They had gone along with the program when starting out and wound up in highly dissatisfying occupations. One person said, "I'm here because I believe there has to be something better."

Of the four categories of response, only the first reflects clear vision and intention. Sadly, only two people in the class gave this kind of response. The other twenty or so people were either confused or making choices based upon what someone else believed they should do. Although this is a clearly unscientific sample, the spread does reflect what I have heard in my twenty or so years in the workplace. Most people are very unclear about why they are working.

We discussed some of the positives in working for business organizations in the first chapter, but those factors (community, relationships, stability, self-worth, group achievement) are rarely the actual motivating factors that lead a person to choose a standard model job. Community is not a motivating factor; the workplace becomes a person's community when he or she discovers the absence of one in their daily lives. Relationships are not a motivating factor, because we usually do not choose our workmates. Continuity and stability are certainly motivating factors for people who have been in the workplace for awhile, but young people entering the job market for the first time have neither the fear of nor the awareness of instability. They haven't made the financial commitments that often tie people to their jobs. The search for self-worth is a motivating factor in everything we do from work to sex, and so we cannot count that in our analysis. Finally, people entering the workforce do not consider the possibility of group achievement, because when we join a company, we go in alone. We meet other people on the way and learn that to get anything done at work we need the help of others, but when a person takes a job, he or she is thinking more about their own contribution and not the potential contributions of others. The question may not be why people choose to work in the corporate world but whether or not they consciously choose it to begin with.

Most careers are accidents, not outcomes based on clear intention. I left college intending to be either a rock-and-roll star or an English teacher and wound up bouncing around from quality assurance to human resources to training. Most of the people I have met over the years have had similar experiences. In a leadership course that I have delivered to over four hundred people, I ask a set of warm-up questions that include, "What was your original career ambition?" The vast majority of answers indicate that people are working in fields with no connection whatsoever to their original goals. It is so rare that a participant will say that he or she is fulfilling their original purpose that I can remember every incident, mainly because the other participants expressed their astonishment as obviously as I did. It has happened exactly twelve times, out of approximately four hundred chances.

"I was only going to be here a year or two while I finished school," said a friend of mine reflecting on thirty years of employment at the same company. He had a degree in anthropology and was at the time a high-level director of an electronics firm. "Well, one thing kinda led to another," said another friend, whose career trajectory had been distracted by a bad early marriage, difficult children and financial constraints. Over the years, I have met countless numbers of frustrated artists and musicians, executives who really wanted to be truck drivers, significant numbers of never-to-be teachers and social workers and a surprisingly large population of stymied architects. A few people who were not doing what they wanted to do said they were getting business experience so that they could open their own company somewhere down the road. Whether any of them have done so is unknown, but my instinct says it is unlikely, particularly if they stay long enough to begin worrying about stability. The point is that most American businesses (and I would expect this applies to most people who work for the government) are populated with folks who are not doing what they really want to do.

It is supposed to be a hallmark of maturity to accept such a fate. "That's the way the world is—get used to it," they'll say. "You're going to have to learn that you can't do everything you want to do," mom and dad would tell us. These messages are more deeply embedded in our collective consciousness than the success slogans manufactured for people with a desperate desire to believe in something. I once worked with a guy who kept a tin can in a prominent position on his desk. It said, "Success comes in cans, not in cannots." We all wish happiness were so easily attainable. In reality, most people believe they cannot, and many people who have attained what this society defines as success are pretty unhappy with their circumstances. Many work themselves out of the possibility of meaningful relationships and burden themselves with the staggering weight of unwanted obligations that accompany success.

So, why are so many people not doing what they want to do? Well, some of it has to do with confidence, some of it has to do with opportunity, but much of it has to do with the power of the expectations of other people.

The Weight of Expectations

Many people suffer from the need to either live up to the expectations of other people or to exceed them in some way. Parents are a great source of this trouble, trying to compensate for their personal sense of failure by heaping expectations of success onto their children. The common expression "I want my children to have a better life than I did" becomes twisted by the pressure parents place on themselves and their children to make that intention real.

My dear mother had that problem. Because dad was pretty much out of the picture most of the time, mom carried the burden of holding the family together. She did pretty well under the circumstances, moving up in her chosen workplace hierarchy through a combination of perseverance and hard work. Still, no matter how much she liked the people she worked with and no matter how important she felt when she went on business trips, she still knew deep down inside that it was "just a job."

Being the only boy in a litter of five during a time when all dreams of success were channeled to the male half of the equation, I was constantly "encouraged" to "be" something. At first, a doctor. Then a lawyer (this was during the Perry Mason era when attorneys were still considered respectable human beings). For a brief time, she wanted me to be a baseball player (at the time, low pay but high status). When I resisted all of these overtures and settled on an English degree, she at least hoped I would turn out to be a university professor. Not being able to stand the rigors of literary research, I went into business instead, fully intending to develop a career in the arts to take me out of the corporate world forever.

My mother never encouraged my artistic side (that was left to my Bohemian male parent), largely because it did not fit in with her notions of success. As things turned out, she would have been thrilled that a combination of poor choices and lack of discipline led me to become successful in the business world, but I do not hold that against her.

I was fortunate that my mother had a good heart and didn't pressure me much. She would back off when I asked her to back off. She only wanted me to be happy. It was just that her conventional idea of happiness (high status job and marrying "a nice girl") did not connect with who I was and what I wanted to be.

If everyone had been lucky enough to have such a kindhearted parent, we would all be better off than we are now. Unfortunately, many parents do not back off, but pressure their children through nagging, sarcastic comments and scarcely veiled threats. This results in what we have today: a society filled with people still trying to prove to their parents that they are worth something. "See, I can do it, mom," is probably the true motto of successful people today. If a parent has been particularly skilled at hooking into the insecurities of their offspring, that only motivates the child to "go one better" and spend their whole lives trying to surpass parental expectations. Life then becomes an essentially fruitless struggle to prove one's worth to somebody who "matters." People motivated in such a way are often the source of the many ethical problems that exist in our society today, because their single-minded motivation encourages them to devalue any apparent obstacle, including the rights of their fellow citizens.

Even people with great parents struggle with expectations, but from a different source. Around the time of high school, the peer group begins to assert its authority over individual choices, creating the motivation to follow the crowd. While this dynamic has been demonstrated to be a major threat to the desire to keep our children drug-free, there is very little protest about the peer pressure that encourages people to get stuck in the rat race. The need to keep up with one's peers in fashion eventually translates into the "need" for cars, homes, vacations to status locations and impressive titles. As mentioned before, when people identify themselves to strangers, they state their occupation first. People who lack status occupations are often dismissed or ostracized (or at least find it difficult to pick up anyone in a bar). Read through the personal ads in your local paper and you will find just as many requests for "professional" and "financially independent" mates than you will for "loving" and "sensitive" people, as if a person's bank account or resumé could guarantee romantic compatibility.

Whether expectations come from parents or from peers, they eventually translate into self-expectations. Little tapes go off in our heads telling us that we should be "better" than we are. They become such a part of our programming that we begin to think the voices are our own. They are not, but the fact that they seem to be leads us to the next cause of winding up in jobs we do not like: the absence of self-purpose.

The Drive to Specialize

Expectations can indeed be powerful enough to wipe clean any self-motivation we may have had. Anyone with a strong sense of purpose will admit that maintaining that purpose against the tide of social expectation is a difficult challenge. The reason they do not give in as easily as the rest of us is that their sense of purpose is clearer and more powerful than the expectations threatening to eat away at their souls. This could point the way to a possible remedy: if one can develop a strong sense of purpose, one can overcome the power of expectations and accomplish what they were set on this earth to accomplish.

Sadly, the answer is not quite so simple. People who are successful are successful because they have focused on the one thing that will make them successful. Once they reach a comfortable status level, they may branch out into other activities, as evidenced by numerous people who have started out as singers and later have moved into film (we will avoid any judgment as to the critical value of such moves). All of our society is geared towards the notion of focus. "Stick to your knitting," comes the advice to business in the pages of *In Search of Excellence*. Degree programs and career centers encourage specialization, not generalization. When people ask children want they want to be, they learn quickly to respond with "the one thing," because that's what we encourage in our culture. They may string several possibilities together with the word "or" but rarely do they combine the professions with the word "and." The cultural norm is you can only be one thing and the other things do not really count. You may be a great musician in your spare time, but you are "really" a marketing analyst, not a musician. You make your money as a marketing analyst, and therefore, that's who you are.

This norm defies human reality. Just as there are some people who have the discipline, tenacity and desire to focus on a single task or field for an entire lifetime, there are some people who get bored with such confines. They don't want to do one thing, they want to do lots of things. They want to write, sing, spend a little time on computer programming and then maybe work a couple of days a week at the local youth club. Or perhaps they want to balance their interest in library work with a little time in the garden. Or most often, they get bored doing the same old thing from year to year, and so every three or five years want to do something completely different. These are usually extremely competent people who could shift from accounting to modern dance with little difficulty.

Unfortunately, they rarely get the chance. First, people who have generalist tendencies are often unsure of themselves, largely because they have no place in society. "Ands" are not allowed; you have to specialize in one profession if you are going to "be successful." The professions themselves encourage this by developing bodies of knowledge translated into degree programs that guarantee that people entering the profession will have to go through a rite of passage initiating them into the secret knowledge of the professional cult. Of course, there are real professions that do require extensive and specific knowledge (medicine comes to mind), but there are several professions that are the result of status inflation. Picking on my own field, I will say unequivocally that the most effective human resources and organizational development people are those with liberal arts or other generalist education behind them, and the least effective are those with degrees in human resources and organizational behavior. When business degrees began appearing at universities in the late nineteenth century, there were vocal protests from those who argued that business was hardly a field of knowledge. While those people (academics, no doubt) may have been motivated by status needs, it is a common human failing to create bodies of knowledge designed primarily to raise status and keep undesirables out. Professional inflation encourages the general belief that our careers should be as monogamous as our marriages, which explains why people with multiple career ambitions are as unwelcome in our society as people who enjoy multiple romantic relationships (always denigrated as "just playing the field").

Because generalists have little validity in society, they feel uncertain. Because they feel uncertain, they suppress their true desires and submit to either parental or peer expectations. The pejorative label "jack of all trades, master of none" is a culturally sanctioned definition of failure. The structure of single-minded professions and single-focus jobs discourages generalists from manifesting their true potential, which in turn leads to some very unhappy people. These are the people who go into organizations believing that anyone in their right minds would want a multi-faceted individual capable of accomplishing diverse tasks only to find themselves trapped in a cubicle poring over computer printouts after they have been "put in their place" by those guarding their precious territories.

The Comfort Trap

As noted before, jobs are still the best opportunity for securing consistent and predictable income. Once we get comfortable with a certain lifestyle, it is hard to give it up for what other people have told us is a "silly dream." Common wisdom takes over for native intelligence and teaches us to dismiss those yearnings as "impractical." People learn to compensate for unrealized ambitions by turning them into hobbies (that they often never have enough time for), or by turning to the numerous mind-numbing experiences offered in our culture, from bad television to sporting rituals to alcohol. When you are safe, secure, eating well and enjoying the odd social event here and there, it is easy to feel comfortable.

However, comfort comes at a price. We often enter into financial obligations driven by our "need" to have things, only to regret it later when an opportunity to get closer to our true desires comes up and we are financially unable to move on it. Taking a full-time job often becomes a web with strands that stretch out to infinity, trapping us in a sticky mess of bills and mortgage payments. Comfort transforms itself into a mess of obligations, and instead of feeling content, we feel restless and stressed out as we realize that we are indeed stuck.

This is not an argument against capitalism or having cool stuff. Nor is it a judgment against people who wish to accumulate possessions. There is nothing wrong with acquiring something that gives us pleasure or is useful to us in some way. There is nothing morally deficient about wanting your kitchen to look nice or feeling like you need to upgrade your video game system. The problem with entering into financial obligations is simply that they limit our ability to make choices. Our drive to *get* often forces us to choose between a limited range of undesirable options, particularly as far as our employment is concerned. With a mortgage and car payment, we become less willing to take risks, even if staying in an unpleasant job or in a crappy organization is draining the spirit.

Some people respond to the pressure created by financial obligations by trying to get ahead of the pack. They work for a promotion, ask for raises, threaten to quit if their demands go unmet. Not only do these strategies rarely work, but even if they do work, they will not solve the problem of financial pressure. Anyone who has received a promotion will tell you that more money means more obligations. It is the rare human being who puts the extra cash aside to invest in their ideals. What happens is that once we get a little breathing room, we buy better stuff, go to more expensive restaurants, buy unnecessary software upgrades and wind up in the same trap we thought we had managed to escape.

The Problem of Self-Confidence

Even when financial obligations seem to have us chained to a particular job or career path, a little creative thinking combined with a financial restructuring package might be able to buy us more freedom. I knew a guy who was doing very well in the conventional sense who got sick and tired of worrying about how he was going to keep up. He sold nearly everything he owned, bought an old VW van and lived in that for a couple of years while saving money to embark on a year-long cross-country journey. His diet consisted of peanut butter sandwiches, apples and water, a culinary sacrifice he deemed necessary to achieving his goal. After two years, he started up the microbus and headed off into the sunset.

Of course, his personal circumstances had a lot to do with his ability to follow his dream. He was without marriage and without children, the two situations that create the most complicated obligations known to humanity. Even so, he managed to get through two years of low-status life (he did not entertain much during that period), resisting every pressure to accumulate things in order to realize his goal. Getting past cultural expectations and pressures is never easy, no matter what your circumstances.

However, the real reason he was able to follow in the footsteps of Lewis and Clark was that he had a strong sense of self. He not only wanted something but he decided he deserved to have it and then had the courage to see it to completion. These are qualities that are missing from the vast majority of people who work for a living.

As we mentioned, many people go into organizations because they are not really sure of what they want. Getting a job in the business world is the default choice for people who are uncertain about their goals, whether that uncertainty is due to having generalist tendencies in a specialist culture or simply not having found something that really grabs them. Life in an organization, with its distorted communication and constant frustration, is hardly the place where one would go to seek clarity. The comfort trap then kicks in, leaving us both confused and stuck at the same time.

It is almost impossible for a confused, stuck person to have much self-confidence. Without self-confidence, it is difficult to make any significant changes in one's life, for confidence gives us the courage to take risks. More painfully, the lack of self-confidence causes us to wonder whether or not it's our fault that we're in the mess we're in. We start blaming ourselves for the stupid choices we made in the past, adding to our stress levels and making us more and more stuck.

Organizations support this cycle by validating the use of blame and guilt as legitimate methods to induce people to display desired behavior. This reflects the norm in the larger culture, where we are far more willing to search for culprits than show compassion for human beings who make mistakes. After experiencing the constant finger-pointing that goes on in most organizations, any confidence we have dissolves into a series of defense strategies designed to ensure survival. People in survival mode do not create new opportunities for themselves. Their primary concern is protecting what they have and after doing battle week in and week out, they are tired, drained and unable to generate possibilities.

Burdened by blame, guilt and obligation, the average person starts to wonder about his or her unhappy circumstances. Most tragically, they start to wonder, "Is it me?" They think that if they could do better, if they could solve this particular problem or please this particular person, that some sense of self-worth will be restored. This is only a temporary solution leading to relief without achievement, and relief is not the best tonic for strengthening sagging self-esteem. The average person counts their blessings, tells themselves they're lucky just to have this job and forgets about any possibility of life beyond the workplace.

What to Do: A Beginning

People often do not stay in organizations because they a fulfilling their heartfelt desires. A combination of cultural expectations, personal uncertainty, the seductiveness of comfort, the weight of obligations and the consequent failure of confidence is why people many people find themselves in organizations. Yes, there are some people in the corporate world who are doing what they want to do, but they are a decided minority. Why else would organizations feel the need to control people? The simple fact is that organizations use control mechanisms because not too many people really want to be there. We are in a situation where a good portion of the people in this country spend the majority of their time doing something they do not want to do, then spend the rest of their time recovering from the energy drain created by doing something that has no connection to their spirit.

Since this was a situation created by human beings and was neither ordained by the gods nor by fortune, this means that human beings can change it. To do so, however, requires a significant shift in our thinking on two fronts.

In the first place, we have to decide as a people that the current situation is unacceptable, that it is morally wrong to build and sustain structures that dehumanize people. We have to demand that businesses change their raison d'être from the single-minded focus on profit to creating workplaces where people have real choices about their lives and about the direction of the business itself. We have to tell government to stop the focus on creating vast amounts of new jobs as if generating millions of meaningless situations was a good thing for people. We have to retrain the people in charge of our education system that their task is not to produce specialized drones to serve the economic engine but to help young people make intelligent and satisfying choices about the directions (emphasis on the plural) they want to explore. We have to stand up for the humanity of the work experience, for the inalienable right of the individual to exercise the opportunity to reach his or her full potential.

I will now climb down from my soapbox. While I meant everything I said in the previous paragraph, I also know that trying to inspire a mass movement for work fulfillment is a hopeless cause. Let me clarify: work fulfillment is indeed a worthy cause. Mass movements are not only notoriously ineffective, but are by their very nature dehumanizing. Large amounts of people engaged in a cause invariably leads to the anonymity of everyone involved. It would be a glaring contradiction (to say the least) for anyone to spark a mass movement in support of the individual employee that turns those employees into statistics.

It also doesn't make any sense to start pointing the finger at "big business" or "government" or anyone else for that matter. The only thing blame ever creates is defensiveness and a war is always harder on the soldiers than it is on the generals. We can take the perspective that we are victims of faceless institutions or we can move in a different direction. The line from The Beatles' "Revolution" demonstrates the underlying truth:

> *You tell me it's the institution,*
> *Well, you know, you'd better free your mind instead.*

If we are going to change the current set of circumstances to increase the quality and quantity of our choices, we will have to rethink the entire problem.

Curiously enough, the answer lies in that thing we all try to avoid: responsibility.

*　　　　　*　　　　　*

Exercise 6: Looking at Choices

Here we look at you arrived at the place you find yourself today. Pull out your notebook and get to work!
1.   What was your original career ambition?
2.   If you are not working in a job that falls within the scope of that original career ambition, what happened?
        —There were no jobs in that field

—I lost interest in that field

—The jobs in that field did not pay well enough

—You know, I really don't know what happened

3. On a scale of 1 to 10, how close are you to doing what you want to be doing, with "1" being "totally disconnected" and "10" being "perfectly in sync?"

4. What are some of the expectations others have placed on you in relation to your choice of occupation?

5. What are some of the expectations you have placed on yourself as to the meaning of success? What do you think you have to do to "be successful?"

6. Which of the following do you see as obstacles to doing what you want to do? Check all that apply:

—The expectations of others

—I am a specialist in a field where demand is low

—I am a generalist in a specialist world

—Financial obligations

—Obligations to other people, family, friends

—My own laziness

—A lack of self-confidence

—Other (describe):

Remember something about these obstacles: they are based on your personal perception of the situation. They may be entirely unreal. We will test their reality in the self-responsibility portion of the book.

Part Two:

Creating Responsible Choices

A New Perspective on Responsibility

The notion of responsibility is one that most Americans find difficult to grasp. Think of the O. J. case, the Bobbits, the British Nanny, President Clinton's various trials and tribulations and you will get a sense of the problem. There is little or no agreement in our society as to what constitutes responsibility.

Part of the problem is that the word responsibility has been contaminated with implications of guilt and blame. This is unfortunate, because when that connotation is combined with a second connotation of no forgiveness, who would willingly accept responsibility for anything?

But the larger part of the problem is that we have confused two separate and distinct notions: responsibility and obligation.

The modern person in any civilized society exists in an ocean of obligations. Many obligations are unwanted, either because they were forced upon us as the outcome of making bad choices or because we have changed our minds and do not want to have the burden anymore. Because unwanted obligations create pressure and stress, we have devised various methods for backing out of them. Our shift in values over the last few decades has given people permission to do the unthinkable as far as meeting commitments are concerned. Bankruptcy no longer carries the stigma it did a few decades ago and there are always lawyers around to help us bend the truth so we can get off the hook for various crimes and misdemeanors. If murderers can mount successful defenses by saying "the Twinkies made me do it," or "my parents made me kill them," then we figure that the system can certainly cut us a little slack when we need it. We can get out of contracts, marriages and any other form of commitment with only the tiniest application of ingenuity. Since we use the word "responsible" to describe our relationship to an obligation, the entire notion of responsibility gets dragged down with it.

However, there is a positive side to responsibility, best demonstrated when we consider the act of bonding ourselves to the little people who cannot make independent choices. I do not know of any good parents who regret having their children. They may regret their career choices or they may have wished that the children had come at a more convenient time, but having children is one obligation most people enjoy, despite the struggles. Yes, there are deadbeat dads and moms, parents who abuse their children in unthinkable ways, and even some who leave their children as orphans or dead. But for the most part, children seem to be an obligation we do not mind as much as some of the others, and we treat them relatively well—not out of law or contract, but just because.

This is in part because children give us hope. We see in our children the existence of possibility, of ideals, of unlimited potential. This helps us compensate for our own sense of failure at not doing what we wanted to do. Our children help us maintain our sanity by reminding us that we are human, a condition sometimes suppressed through the daily toil. We need our children just as much as they need us and so we willingly sacrifice our true ambitions to put food on the table and to get them through college.

However, we may not need to sacrifice ourselves for the good of our children, for often that form of sacrifice is merely a convenient excuse that allows us to avoid taking risks. Children by nature are pretty forgiving, particularly before they become teenagers and begin viewing their parents either as the enemy or a walking automatic teller machine. Most children want their parents to be happy and do not have the same financial demands that their parents have. In truth, many of the financial obligations that come out of parenting have nothing to do with what the child wants but with what we think they should want or with what will raise our status within our peer group. Peer groups of parents are often the worst peer groups, creating standards of dress, education and activity that other parents are expected to emulate, often at significant cost. This in turn extends the financial web even further and as we look at our personal budgets and plan for the future, we tell ourselves "only five more years," repeating what we told ourselves five years before.

What happens in our relationship with children is that we transform a natural responsibility into an obligation by contaminating the relationship with our own insecurities. Our innate desire to respond effectively to our children is transformed into a chore through the heavy expectations we place on our children.

The perceptive reader will note we are making a very important distinction here. Obligation is not the same thing as responsibility. Responsibilities are welcomed. Obligations are not. Responsibility comes from within, obligation from without. Responsibility is a motivator. Obligations are demotivators. Responsibility is a source of personal empowerment. We often accumulate obligations for the opposite reason: so we can stop ourselves from doing what we really want to do.

If you think that this makes no sense at all—I mean, why would any sane person stop themselves from doing what they really want to do?—then you are entirely right. It makes no sense whatsoever. Rational beings would do everything they could to give themselves the opportunity to do exactly what they want to do.

Then again, we are dealing with *human* beings, which is not the same thing as rational beings.

The Difference between Responsibility and Obligation

Ah, responsibility. The meaning of this word has been so convoluted by a society completely fixated on the need to blame that it is difficult to mention it without running into the danger of turning people off. Nonetheless, we will ignore the risks and forge ahead, largely because understanding responsibility in its true meaning is the key to making conscious and satisfying life choices.

We define responsibility as the choice to respond effectively to a person or situation. What makes a response effective is how well it reflects the values and needs of self, others and community. Responsibility differs from obligation in the source and power of its motivation.

Obligations are specific agreements that people enter into as the result of transactions. If I sell you a computer, I am obliged to give you the computer in exchange for the sum we have negotiated. If I am a computer manufacturer, I have an obligation to follow various regulations in the manufacture of that computer so that it doesn't blow up when the customer flips the switch. Obligations are contained in rules, regulations, contracts and laws. They are limitations we agree to because we believe we will get something in return. We agree to obey the law to avoid having to go to jail. We agree to marry so-and-so because we think that person will make us happy. Obligations arise from the need for social order, and as such, they are often enforced by the authorities.

Responsibilities, on the other hand, work on a deeper level than obligations. I may be fully aware of a restraining order against the demonstration scheduled for Saturday, but something else motivates me to participate anyway. In this case, that something else is the sense of personal responsibility, captured in the phrase "to thine own self be true." While we will explain this and the other two major responsibilities of life later on, it is sufficient for now to say that the motivation for living up to a responsibility comes from within, not from without. I live up to my obligations out of fear of punishment, a bad credit rating, or fear of a lawsuit. I live up to my responsibilities because I choose to do so out of my own free will. I live up to my obligations because I traded my free will for a specific result. We act purposefully when we are responsible. We act automatically when meeting obligations.

Let's apply this to our relationship with our children. First, although I may spin endless strands of obligations as the result of having children, there is something that motivates me to care for them that is more compelling than the need to stay out of financial trouble. I am driven to respond to them, and even though it may mean giving up a trip to Europe or a new utility vehicle, I don't mind it as much. It is in the essence of the human experience of creating and caring for offspring that bonds are created, bonds that we do not struggle against, bonds that are not restraints but tangible connections with other human beings. No contract is created when I have a child, but something inside compels me to do the best I can for them. I may regret the obligations, but I do not regret the responsibility and the learning that comes from accepting that responsibility.

Responsibility, then, is something created from our essential humanity. It comes from love and not from fear. It comes from the desire to grow as opposed to the need to survive. Responsibility grows from the inner human need to find one's calling, one's offering to life, and not the expectation-driven need to find out where we stand in the pecking order.

Before we go any further, it is important to note that the difference between responsibility and obligation does not excuse you from meeting the latter. As we will see, obligation is an important component of the third level of responsibility, the responsibility to community. Additionally, it never makes sense in the long run to weasel out of an obligation because it usually isn't worth the hassle. The critical point is that responsibility is a far more powerful motivator than obligation. We can escape creditors if we choose to do so, but we can never escape ourselves.

In general, therefore, heed the following:

Consider your obligations well, but embrace your responsibilities.

The Three Basic Responsibilities

Human beings have three basic responsibilities: responsibility to self, responsibility to others and responsibility to the community.

Responsibility to self is basically being true to yourself. It means following your inner drive to manifest yourself in your own unique way. It is not self-indulgence, although the enjoyment of pleasurable things is not to be dismissed as a source of spiritual nourishment or judged as "selfish." If you limit your actions to only the self-indulgent, then it is highly unlikely you are being true to yourself or living up to your other responsibilities. Then again, if you never indulge yourself, you will suffer the consequences of excessive self-repression. "Sooner murder an infant in his cradle than nurse an unacted desire," Blake tells us, arguing that human desire is itself innocent and only made ugly, sick and distorted through years of self-repression. Balance is the key to living up to this and the other two responsibilities.

Responsibility to others means being responsive and respectful to those you know personally. This includes your family, your friends, your workmates, and your neighbors. Responsibility to others does not mean that you have to live up to their expectations or sacrifice yourself to make them happy. Again, balance is critical in living up to the responsibilities of life, and focusing on one at the expense of the other is always a self-destructive act. Responsibility to others involves working together to fulfill mutual needs, the defining quality of any successful relationship. It also means a fundamental respect for human life, including respecting the right of others to make their own choices, as long as those choices do not harm others.

Responsibility to the community is the most difficult of the three because it is the most challenging. This is because in modern society, the definition of community is changing. It used to mean your hometown; now the word can have global implications. Furthermore, communities are by nature fragmented because they are sprouting up all over the place as the result of technological advances. Most of us belong to many communities, from our neighborhood to our poetry circles to our Internet newsgroups. Simply put, a community is a group of people who have chosen to come together out of common interests. This means that for most of us in modern society the workplace is our primary community, for it is the community to which we contribute the greatest amount of time and effort.

Again, it is important that all three responsibilities be attended to in order for a person to feel right with the world. That doesn't mean that we have to be in perfect balance all the time to be happy. What it means is that over time, we feel better when we nourish all three responsibilities. Sometimes you have to go off somewhere for self-reflection, so at that particular moment you are probably being more responsible to self than to others or to the community. Don't worry, you can make it up later by attending to your other responsibilities in time.

I should also clarify that this is not intended to be a framework for happiness. Being responsible will not guarantee that you will always get what you want and that everything will work out. There is nothing on earth that can guarantee you that. This framework is designed to help people process decisions, possibilities and opportunities by making them more understandable. The logic behind this is simple: if we understand the potential consequences of choices, we can make more effective choices. This is not to say that every choice will be effective, for there are always unpredictable variables in anything we do. What the framework does is permit you to make fully conscious choices instead of simply following the program or responding to the various guilt trips being heaped on you from all sides.

Responsibility is the key to making fully conscious choices.

Choices

"Back up a minute!" you say. "You said that a community was a group of people who have chosen to come together. I didn't choose to work at this dump! I came here because I needed a job and this was the only place hiring! Don't tell me I belong to this community—I don't want any part of it!"

Sigh. I hear this kind of thing all the time when I go into organizations. It is a convenient way of distancing oneself from the truth, an easy way to avoid responsibility. It is also absolute, utter nonsense.

Examine the choices. What makes you think you "needed a job?" If you respond that you needed money to survive, any criminal, gambler or con artist will tell you that there are plenty of ways to make money without having to take a job. "Oh, I couldn't do that—that would be wrong!" you gasp. No, I say, you chose not to go into crime because you accepted the responsibility you have to the larger community of civilized society, but that was your choice. "Well, then, what was I supposed to do?" you plead. Well, there are perfectly legal ways of making money, believe it or not. You could have started a business, borrowed money from relatives, sold cars or clothes, moved to another city where the job market was more promising. "But I can't do those things! I have family here and I can't just leave! I don't know how to start a business, my relatives are broke, I don't have a car to sell and all the clothes I have could fit into a carry-on."

Hmm. This sounds serious. Let me see…no, everything still comes down to a choice:

Excuse:	I can't leave the family.
Response:	Many people can't stand their biological families and put as much distance between them and their relatives as possible. No, that's clearly your choice.
Excuse:	I don't know how to start a business.
Response:	You may have a better case by saying you lack the funds to start the business, but I would probably respond that your lack of funds may be in part caused by previous choices that were none too wise. Not knowing how always suggests a choice, because people for the most part are capable of learning new things all the time.
Excuse:	My relatives are broke.
Response:	Well, you have me there, but that's only one out of three.

Excuse: No car, no clothes.

Response: Well, I don't want you to sell what little you have, but it
             was still an option (obviously you didn't have high quality
             options available to you, but they were still options
             nonetheless).

The truth is that of course we choose to work in organizations. Since
one of the fundamental violations of any of the three responsibilities is
avoiding the truth, we are not serving ourselves by denying it. We deny it
in part because we hate to admit that we compromised our dreams to take
a job. We don't want to face the fact that our choice was more of a default
than a fully informed decision. We certainly hate to admit that we made a
mistake. However, failing to admit mistakes is ultimately disempowering
because you never learn from them. Accepting your choice gives you room
to maneuver, because instead of wasting all your time complaining, you
become responsible for doing something for yourself or even for the community. That choice is, of course, up to you.

However, the whole issue of choice is not as simple as saying "everything
is chosen, so grow up and live with it." Whenever you hear a politician or
a business executive complain that "people don't accept personal responsibility" for their lives, what you're really hearing is an attempt by those self-
proclaimed leaders to avoid responsibility themselves. The responsibility
they are trying to avoid is their responsibility to other human beings, and
that avoidance is always given away by the astonishing lack of compassion
these leaders display.

How many times have you made a stupid decision or avoided making
one altogether? Lots of times, I'll bet. I know I have. It is a common
human weakness to shrink back from the precipice, to restrain ourselves
from making a commitment to act. One of the greatest tragedies in the
English language, *Hamlet*, deals with this common human failing. Jerry
Harvey has demonstrated that "action anxiety" is a primary cause of inef-

fective decision-making, as people withhold their true opinions from each other out of fear of real or imagined consequences.

We are all capable of the occasional dumb move. Therefore, it is astonishing to me that some people are more than willing to jump on another person caught making the dumb move or has become paralyzed at the moment of truth. Who are these people to judge us for our failings? Are they so above human failings that they have the right to condemn us? All they are doing in haranguing people about personal responsibility is pointing the finger of blame at another source (welfare mothers, to cite a recent example) to cover up their own failings. It is a psychological shell game and many people fall for it.

It doesn't help anyone to shout, "You Are Responsible!" in a thunderous voice from the mountaintop. It doesn't help anyone to say, "you made the choice—tough shit," and walk away. We have a responsibility to our fellow human beings to help them through their thinking when making choices, and an even greater responsibility to show empathy and compassion when they wind up making a mess of things. This does not mean that we have to tolerate people who choose to act in an abusive manner or forgive unforgivable acts like murder or rape. As much as I would like to emulate the great people of history who have taken forgiveness to unthinkable levels, I would find it extremely difficult to forgive certain actions that violate the sanctity of human life. Nonetheless, we could all be more forgiving with each other regarding the choices we make that result in minor or easily fixable harm to self or others and we can certainly afford to put ourselves in the chooser's shoes when they are faced with a difficult dilemma.

Accountability 101

Corporations have always had problems with responsibility because in a corporation it usually means "the right to nail somebody's ass if they screw up." This definition is manifested in the corporate synonym, "accountability." This term has financial overtones, which reveals part of the problem. Corporations use the words "responsible" and "accountable" more for ease of classification than as a mechanism for discerning the truth. The logic is that if I know what person is accountable for which action, it allegedly helps organize my people much like a spreadsheet organizes my figures. It also makes leaders feel better when they can identify who is accountable because not only does it make things nice and tidy, but provides them with an easily identifiable scapegoat if any shit should hit the corporate fan.

This is an all-too-typical example of organizations trying to simplify matters by ignoring the contradictions in the logic. It's sort of like, "if we believe it, it must be true." In this case, the identification of an accountable individual is not only wasteful but also inaccurate. All work in any organization is by nature collaborative, so if the intent is to round up and punish the guilty, corporations should prepare themselves for mass executions whenever a mistake is made. Further, individual accountability is usually divorced from the learning process, so instead of taking the truly responsible action of helping an alleged non-performer think things through, management resorts to blame, blame, blame.

A friend of mine who worked at yet another one of those "best managed companies" had a terrible experience with corporate accountability. Essentially the company lied to her about what the job was all about. When she arrived on site, she discovered she was "responsible" for two additional functions that were not even discussed in the interview. They also assured her that she had a fully trained staff. She found out that none of her people knew the slightest thing about their jobs beyond what they read in outdated corporate procedures. Brought on board to fix a critical operational issue, she found herself working eighty-plus hours a week to try to get a handle on it. Finally, she realized that she couldn't repeat Hitler's mistake in the war with the Soviet Union and try to take Moscow and Leningrad at the same time. So she went to her boss with hard data clearly supporting the need to put a couple of projects on hold until the top-priority crisis had passed.

The boss responded in a memo (although his office was but fifty feet away), in which he copied his boss and a couple of other corporate representatives. He denied her request with the "if I believe it, it must be true" thinking that captures the essence of corporate accountability. He rejected her proposal. He ignored the data. He reminded her that she was accountable for the total function and that she had better figure out a way to get things done. Dismissing her double-overtime contribution to date, he said to her, "Effort doesn't count. Only results matter."

How utterly helpful. Instead of trying to assist his employee, who through her tireless efforts demonstrated a clear commitment to fixing the problem, this so-called leader cut her off with a reminder of her "accountability" and a memo designed primarily to cover his ass. When she went back to him and attempted to at least get his support in gaining some help and cooperation from the other managers (who were in fact causing the problem she was hired to solve), he cut her off and reminded her once again that she was accountable.

To say that this leader made a choice not to respond effectively to the situation would be an understatement. He was neither responsible to her or to his organization by insisting on "accountability." He may have believed that reciting this magic word over and over again would make a difference, and that if he believed in it strongly enough, the results he wanted would appear before his very eyes.

Pretty silly. His employee quit two weeks later.

Our heroine had decided to be responsible to herself first and refused to become a martyr to the hopeless cause of corporate accountability. To get to that point, though, she put herself through a phenomenal amount of stress and aggravation caused by a blockhead of a manager. For a while, she wavered between her responsibility to herself and her responsibility to the workplace community. When it became clear that she could live up to neither responsibility, she moved on to bigger and better things.

Responsibility Conflicts

The story illustrates an important truth. Sometimes one or more of the three responsibilities appear to be in conflict with each other. This shows up often in intimate relationships. For example, I feel the need to go off for two weeks to meditate in the woods, my lover may claim that I am not being particularly responsible to her by leaving her alone for a fortnight. I might respond that the two weeks will make me a better and more responsive person, to which she may respond, "Well, can't you become a better person around me?" Eventually, if our values are congruent, we will find a balance that satisfies our needs.

However, the most problematic conflict of all is one between responsibility to self and responsibility to community. Often the community demands conformance as a condition of membership and the requirements of conformance are frequently in conflict with individual conscience. This struggle between personal and social truths has been the subject of much great literature and several fine films. We root for the lone individual standing up against the obtuse forces in the community; often, though, the individual winds up dead (*Easy Rider*), lobotomized (*One Flew Over the Cuckoo's Nest*) or drops out of the community altogether (anything by Kerouac).

Dropping out is certainly an option many people use to escape conformist pressures. The Catholic Church has lost many adherents due to their views on women and abortion; I dropped out of the one professional organization because I felt they were only interested in spreading their peculiar dogma. However, there are certain community pressures that are very difficult to avoid, and so a permanent state of tension arises between self and community that can become very uncomfortable.

Take, for example, a lesbian mother with a nose piercing who has come out. This is a person who has made a choice to be true to herself against powerful social pressures to conform to the heterosexual norm. Being a mother and a lesbian at the same time adds to the pressure, for there are millions of so-called Christians (and you thought Christianity was based on forgiveness?) for whom such a situation is intolerable, even if it is fundamentally none of their goddamn business in a country that is supposed to have separation of church and state. The nose piercing limits her choices in terms of which employers will hire her, for there are very few communities who prohibit discrimination on the basis of personal appearance. If she is in any way public with her affections, she runs the risk of inciting a gay basher.

She may have made the choice to keep things secret, and many people whose norms differ from the social standard choose to construct a façade to survive in the larger community. Neither choice is "wrong" just as neither choice is "right." There are trade-offs and consequences associated with each, and it is not for us to stand in judgment of any individual making such a difficult decision. For the most part, though, it is always better to be true to yourself than to deny yourself, for the simple reason that you cannot truly live up to your other responsibilities while living a lie. Lies eat away at people, distorting them and making them less than they are.

It is possible to find a reasonable balance in such a difficult situation. Perhaps our mother could choose to come out to a limited circle of supportive people—an alternative community—while deciding that her sexual choice is irrelevant outside of that circle. The truism still holds even in this situation: all of us must find outlets for self-expression and self-validation or our other responsibilities become meaningless. Friends and family get only a shadow of a person; our communities are denied the energy we choose to repress. "To thine own self be true" becomes an overriding consideration in discussing responsibility, always bounded by the natural law that in being one's true self, one cannot and should not bring harm to other people.

In terms of the workplace, many of us have experienced the conflict between personal and organizational values. Most of the time we swallow our anger or release it over time in gripe sessions. We rarely challenge the organization's truths beyond a few sarcastic snipes at the leadership. This is partly because of the universal tendency to discount our own opinions when they seem to be at odds with the larger group. It is also partly due to executive fear of dissension within the ranks, which translates into the control mechanisms we discussed earlier. "We want everyone on the same page," goes the rational argument, but if getting everyone on the same page means sacrificing healthy debate and neglecting genuine concerns, everyone suffers. The organization is denied viewpoints that can expand its ability to perceive alternatives. The individual is denied the opportunity to test his or her ideas out on a larger audience.

This conflict is not going to be solved without a shift in values that places responsibility to human beings on an equal level with profit and productivity. Such a shift would represent a massive change in our thinking, to be sure. The extent of the change required seems so intimidatingly vast that it is easy to assume that "things will never change." Underneath that assumption is the even more erroneous belief that change of this magnitude can only start from the top, where the power resides.

Contrary to conventional wisdom, change does not begin at the top. The people on top are inherently conservative, in part because they want to protect what they have and in part because they need to ensure the continuity of the organization. Those in power usually change only when the circumstances demand that they change in order to survive. These circumstances appear when enough pressure accumulates below and around them to get their attention. However, the pressure is not built by magic. All change begins in the individual conscience and in the individual's belief that things can and should be different. Once the individual human being shares the possibilities with others, it starts a chain of perception-shifting that activates the power that moves organizations and societies.

But it all starts with the individual, and responsible individuals act when change is needed.

Since up to this point we have only described the three responsibilities in general terms, we will now outline the specific actions that support them.

Responsibility to Self

Responsibility to self is based on being true to oneself. This is achieved through four actions:

Self-reflection: This is the old Socratic suggestion, "Know thyself." It is impossible to have any sense of self without having some idea of who you are. Self-reflection is an ongoing process because people change and grow over time, and as much as we value the person who "knows what he or she wants," this is often a façade designed to mask inner uncertainty. If you find yourself uncertain, confused by inner contradiction and discovering new things about yourself all the time…congratulations, you're a human being!

Self-maintenance: To live up to your responsibility to self, you have to nurture that self so that it can survive and grow. This is not as easy as our health-conscious (some would say health-fascist) culture would like you to believe. For a long time I have kept a newspaper clipping of an Associated Press article about a Jordanian woman who allegedly lived to be 165 years old. The report says she "lived a normal life, smoked cigarettes, had a strong body and excellent memory and ate half a sheep a day." Hardly the regimen prescribed for us by the American Medical Association. We have had so many contradictory studies published by alleged experts that it is difficult to know the truth about what is good for you (and I don't care what anyone says, no one is going to tell me that chocolate isn't good for my spirits). You have a body and a soul to take care of, so balance the two by determining what works for you to maintain physical and psychological health. I think the real truth is that every body is different just as every soul is different, and you have to experiment to see what works for you. Self-maintenance is all about making a conscious effort to pay attention to the need to balance body and soul instead of ignoring either completely.

Self-development: Part of your responsibility to yourself involves learning and development. When people try to limit learning through commitment to old dogma or outdated knowledge, they may think they are protecting themselves but what they are really doing is ensuring their self-destruction. Every person, regardless of age, has a responsibility to continue to nurture the intellect through ongoing education. This does not necessarily mean institutionalized education, for often the official channels offer less learning than what you can pick up on your own. Self-development means staying sharp, honing your craft and expanding into new areas. The process can include travel, reading, conversation or classroom experiences. Self-development is a critical part of both self-responsibility and responsibility to the community.

Self-forgiveness: Most people are terribly hard on themselves. I suffer from this affliction, accepting responsibility for anything and everything that goes on around me, beating myself up into a pulp after I've made a mistake or hurt someone's feelings. It is harder to forgive yourself when people are pointing fingers at you, but unless you develop this skill you will constantly find yourself painted into a psychological corner. We need to learn and move on from our constant mistakes, and we need to learn to live with ourselves in the process.

Responsibility to Others

Responsibility to others is all about your personal relationships and doing the things you need to do to keep them healthy. There are five fundamental actions related to this responsibility:

Seek the true self: Many people enter relationships based on their personal expectations of what they want the other person to be. This is obviously true in many romantic encounters, but also applies to the workplace, where we heap expectations on leaders and co-workers as to how they should behave. Such a perspective is inherently unfair and invariably disappointing, because no one is here on this earth to live up to our expectations. To be truly responsible to others, we must release others from our expectations and establish a space where people are encouraged to be natural. This also validates and supports the self-responsible action of self-development, in that by letting go of our projections, we learn more about others and therefore ourselves.

Respect for Choices: Along with seeking the real person behind the expectations, it is necessary to learn to accept another person's right to choose. This does not mean that if someone chooses to shoot you that you should let them go ahead and do it, for you would be violating your overriding responsibility to yourself. What it means is that you allow people the right to make choices and mistakes, just as you permit yourself the right to make similar choices (and similar mistakes). It also means practicing tolerance for choices that may not fit with your particular tastes, but as long as a choice brings no harm to another, you cannot interfere. It is up to the person making the decision to judge whether or not a choice will result in harm to him or herself.

Offering Assistance with Choices: Respecting another person's right to make choices does not mean you should simply throw your hands up and back out of the situation. All of us need help in sorting out choices. Sometimes we miss potential consequences or fail to take certain variables into account. We can help others by sharing information and by listening to their thinking. Sharing information and listening without bias are probably the two greatest gifts we can give someone who is facing a difficult choice. Keep in mind that assistance does not involve giving advice or finding other sneaky ways to try to force them to live up to your expectations. It means being there for them, not for you.

Defining Your Parameters: It is important to be fair to others, and being fair often involves explaining to another person your own personal limitations. If your partner wants to be covered in Jell-O but you find the thought distasteful, you should let your partner know before they rush off to the grocery store. On a more serious note, you have to let people know what values are important to you so they can make choices as to how to relate to you. It is not fair to another person for you to withhold values and feelings when withholding that information could lead them to make unwise choices about how they interact with you.

Forgiveness: Just as we need to learn to forgive ourselves, we need to avoid beating up other human beings who engage in the ultimate human experience of screwing up. Your parameters will determine how much you can forgive, which is why it is wise to let the people close to you know just how far your tolerance goes. It is also possible to forgive someone while at the same time deciding that you really don't think it's a good idea to maintain the relationship. In this case, forgiving another is important for you in terms of letting go as it is for the other in terms of receiving permission to attempt change.

Responsibility to Community

The specific responsibilities we adopt in support of a community will vary with the particular community; however, there are four greater responsibilities that will apply to any of them:

Making the Commitment: Except for sociopaths and a few other unique types, human beings have a need to contribute to something larger than themselves. This is why working in an organization can be so frustrating; there seem to be endless obstacles that get in the way of making this important contribution. When you choose to join any community, you have a responsibility to that community to make an honest attempt to improve its circumstances. It may not always work out, but the attempt is what is important. Working in a larger community means working with conflicting goals and desires, because people in the community have varying perspectives on what is best for all. Giving up at the first sign of trouble is hardly a responsible action. When you join a community, you take on partial responsibility for its problems, which means you need to exercise patience and perseverance in pursuing resolution. This validates the self-development responsibility because there is hardly a greater opportunity for skill-building than the complex problems presented by organizational life, be it in the neighborhood or in the workplace.

Supporting the Members: Another responsibility of a community member is to watch out for the best interests of his or her fellows, largely by giving help when asked and by sharing knowledge and relevant information that can strengthen the community and its members (imagine that in the workplace!). When you join a community, you can no longer allow self-interest to be your primary motivation. The needs of the community must also be considered along with your needs when making a decision that will affect you or the larger community. While these needs are often in conflict, it is not always necessary to choose one over the other. People tend to give up too easily and then shrug their shoulders and say, "What can I do?" A responsible person will search long and hard for solutions that meet the needs of most, if not all, of the people in the community.

Meeting Obligations: Your obligations are sometimes made to the other people you know, but most often our obligations involve the powers that be: banks, bill collectors, the State. A responsible person meets his or her obligations for two reasons. It is hardly being responsible to place yourself in the energy-draining situation of avoiding an obligation through legal or illegal means. Second, there is the moral urgency of doing what you say you are going to do when you make a contract. This does not mean that you have to continue in a loveless marriage or keep the lemon you bought until you have finished paying it off. It means that you seek civilized remedies for such situations so that your integrity does not suffer in the process. Largely this involves avoiding the desire to blame the person with whom you are entangled and accepting the truth that you are both equally responsible for the situation. You accept the new set of circumstances (I'm broke, I don't love you anymore, etc.) and together decide what to do about it. Since it is difficult to negotiate with the State about anything, the best advice there is to keep your nose clean and to carefully consider the consequences before entering into any obligation.

Quit When It's Time: This is an aspect of responsibility most people avoid through various rationalizations. The best approach is contained in the following bit of wisdom:

> *You've got to know when to hold 'em,*
> *Know when to fold 'em,*
> *Know when to walk away,*
> *Know when to run.*

When you have nothing left to give to a community, or when your level of frustration exceeds your desire to contribute, leave. If you find yourself blaming everyone around you and sidestepping responsibilities, move on. Admit that you do not belong there and find another community more suited to you. Too many people stay too long in untenable situations out of a lack of self-confidence or a misguided belief that they can somehow turn things around. Learn to back off your personal vision long enough to take an objective look at your relationship with your community, and do yourself a favor by getting out while the getting is good.

Summary

We have now summarized the responsibility framework, describing responsibility to self, to others and to the community. The upcoming chapter on self-responsibility will give you an opportunity to explore directions and your potential for moving closer to doing what you want to do. The exercises in the next chapter are more extensive than those that have appeared in the book so far, because self-responsibility is the foundation of everything else.

Good luck!

Self-Responsibility

The first action one has to take in becoming responsible is to attend to the person closest to home: y-o-u.

This is not an endorsement of the "me-first" mentality. It is the simple acknowledgment of the truth that until you get your stuff together, you will not be able to help anyone else or contribute to your community. Putting aside the argument as to whether self-indulgence is a good or bad thing, the core issue of self-responsibility is learning to escape from the influence of the expectations of others, whether those expectations encourage hedonism or self-sacrifice. The first step in becoming self-responsible is to commit an entirely original act in our mass-market culture: to discover what it is you really want.

What follows are a series of self-guided exercises designed to help you discover just that. Implicit in these exercises is that there is no judgment attached to what you want. If you want to be a struggling artist and risk making no money at all, fine. If you want to grow up to be the richest man or woman on the planet, fine. The other two equally important responsibilities to others and to your communities will discipline and channel your energies away from pure self-indulgence. Do not judge your impulses at this point, for if you repress yourself now, you will never get to the core of what you want to do, and will therefore be more likely to wind up doing something that is not really what you want. That isn't fair to you or anyone else.

Enough said. The next thirty-six pages of this book are yours to write.

*   *   *

Self Responsibility Exercises

These exercises are designed to develop the four aspects of responsibility to self:

Self-reflection
Self-maintenance
Self-development
Self-forgiveness

There are eight phases in this process:

Phase 1:	Do Nothing
Phase 2:	Find Yourself in Memories
Phase 3:	Create Choices
Phase 4:	Define Purposes
Phase 5:	Face the Challenges
Phase 6:	Planning for Balance
Phase 7:	Sacrifices
Phase 8:	Commitments

You have several options as to how to approach these exercises. I suggest you read through them first and then choose which option works best for you:

1. The preferred option is to take one or two weeks off and go to a place that makes you feel good. This will give you sufficient time for both self-reflection and planning.
2. You also have the option of shortening the time based on your own estimate of how long you think you need to work through the process.
3. For those of you who cannot get away, another possibility is to stay home and work through the exercises at a rate of two hours

per night. If you choose this course, make a clear break between the workday experience and the reflective experience by either taking a nap or doing something equally restful between the end of the workday and the start of these exercises.

There are no doubt other choices available to you based on your personal circumstances and limitations. Whatever option you choose, make sure you establish a regular rhythm in completing the process, coming back to the material every day in an environment where you will be free of distractions.

Phase 1: Do Nothing

The saying from the *Tao Te Ching* is "Do nothing and there is nothing that will not be done." In our activity-oriented world, we tend to feel guilty for sitting around and doing absolutely nothing.

However, if you are going to do some serious thinking about yourself and the directions you want to take, you need to make a temporary break with the normal flow of your life. That is why the first thing you need to do is to go someplace where you will be free to do absolutely nothing for a few days.

When I say nothing, what I mean is avoiding any activity that causes you to worry. Limit your activities to things that let your mind wander or that fill your thoughts with images other than the reality of your daily existence. When I want to space out for awhile, I might play video games or I might just sleep. My significant other likes to put her personal belongings in order. Do whatever is restful for you: watch old *I Love Lucy* episodes, play golf, whittle, tinker, go to museums, play the drums, whatever.

You may even want to consider things you used to do in your childhood before you started feeling guilty about how childish they might appear. I remember spending hours at my grandmother's house in the summer sitting in a field near the train tracks and spending the entire day counting the number of cars on the trains that passed by. That might seem a silly thing for an adult to do, but that is because adults often feel they have to justify every minute of their time as either being useful or impressive. For this exercise, you need to let all of that go and do whatever you need to do to rest your weary soul.

As far as selecting a place, go to a place that makes you feel good just to be there. For some people, this is a natural setting like the woods or the beach. For others, like Cousin Vinny, it's a noisy place like a big city (I suggest you avoid prison, though). My idea of tranquility is sometimes the ocean, sometimes Manhattan. I remember going to Paris once on a frequent flyer ticket and spending most of my ten days there sleeping in my hotel room because it felt so right to be there.

Count on doing nothing for a couple of days, then you can go on to the next exercise. Note: for those of you who choose the stay-at-home option, schedule this first step for a weekend, preferably a long weekend.

Tip:

One question you'll have to answer is whether or not you want to go alone on this little journey into nothingness. Well, remember that the purpose is for you to suspend day-to-day existence so you can get away from the expectations and pressures other people place on you. This need would tend to favor a solo journey.

On the other hand, there are people who can't stand being alone and the anxiety of loneliness is not conducive to tranquility. I know I feel that way sometimes, especially if I'm alone in a hotel room (the result of too many business trips). If you do choose to take someone along, explain what you're doing and why, then negotiate some free space and time where you can be away from that person to let your mind go.

Exercise: Preparing to Do Nothing

1.   Identify three places where you can go that make you feel good about being there:

2.   List three activities that you can do while you are there that will disconnect your mind from present worries:

3.   Schedule the time you need to complete the exercises, beginning with at least two days of mental nothingness:

4.   Prepare a message to your significant other, children, workmates or others to guarantee that they will leave you alone for two weeks (if that's what you choose) or give you the space during your home time to complete the exercises. Here is a suggested format:

"I've been doing a lot of thinking lately about my career and I really need some time to get my thoughts together. I'm going to take a couple of weeks off to sort things out for myself. I'd really appreciate it if you would give me the gift of this free time and wish me good luck. I'll leave a number, but I would appreciate it if you would only use it in an emergency.

"Trust me to work things out and come back in better spirits. I really appreciate this."

Your message:

*   *   *

Doing Nothing: What to Bring

Whether you choose to go somewhere or stay at home and lock the doors, you're going to want to bring a few things with you. Some of these things are designed to enhance your personal comfort and security; others will be used in later phases of the process. Feel free to make your own choices in this regard; however, stay away from anything or anyone that comes with attached expectations or pressures.

Collect these for later phases:
    Photo albums with childhood and family pictures.

Photo albums with vacation pictures (but only if you really had a good time).

A small bag (no larger than a carry-on) of personal memorabilia that is meaningful to you and has the power to trigger memories.

Three items that help you relax. For me, nothing beats a good bottle of bubble bath; other people relax while listening to Oasis at full volume on a Discman. Whatever works for you.

Collect these for personal comfort and security:

Your pet, if your pet travels. Pets give unconditional love more effectively than most, if not all, human beings.

Your favorite music—A book if you need to read to go to sleep (avoid this instruction if you are thinking about being a writer, for the danger of anxiety may be too great).

Clothes that make you feel good. If you feel good in tight leather pants, no one is going to judge you. Some people feel good in old clothes; other people feel better when they look their best, even if the clothing itself is not particularly comfortable. A mix is perfectly acceptable.

The usual travel stuff, being careful not to violate any of the guidelines that follow.

Try to bring as little as humanly possible. Now I know that it is difficult for many people to do without their stuff, but the less you end up with the better off you'll be. Remember, the objective of doing nothing is to clear your mind of all the expectational clutter that has been filling it up for years. Possessions themselves may create expectational associations, so approach this as a minimalist.

If you stay at home, clean up the house and put the usual junk in its place before you begin doing nothing.

What Not to Bring

In general, you should avoid anything that has expectations, judgments or depressing memories attached to it. You want things that will help you get in touch with your true desires, not things that will force you into compromise before you've even begun. This list consists of the people and things you may want to leave behind in order to give yourself room to grow:

Your spouse. Let's start off with a little controversy! Other than the workplace, there is no human experience that one enters into with more expectations than marriage. People who have lived together for years sometimes change unpredictably once they've tied the knot. Many men and women spend their youth dreaming about the ideal spouse long before they actually meet that special someone, which means they go into the arrangement with strong beliefs as to how that special someone should behave. If you are going to change your path or discover your true desires, you need to be free of what anyone, including your spouse, thinks you should be.

Your significant other. Marriage isn't the only place where heavy expectations are created. Any people who have lived together for a long time can develop the same problem. If you have a significant other (or even a spouse) who is completely in support of whatever direction you choose to take, even if it means cutting your income by 90% for two years while you go study Peruvian ruins, then ignore this instruction (especially if your partner can be a valuable friend during the later phases).

Your appointment book. Get away from anything work-related and anything having to do with a schedule.

Your cell phone or pager. Cellular phones and other mobile telecommunications devices are definitely verboten for two reasons. One, you don't want to go to a place where you feel an overwhelming urge to show how important you are by whipping out your cell phone, for that is the world you're trying to escape. Second, you don't want anyone to have access to you on their terms. This is your time and you need to celebrate it. If you're staying at home, consider unplugging the jack for a few days (but make sure you can plug it back in quickly in case of emergency).

Unfinished projects. Right now you need to get away from all anxieties. Your unfinished projects may tend to remind you of failure, which in turn can reduce your confidence. Leave unfinished artwork or craft projects at home unless they help you relax and you have a pretty good track record of finishing things.

          *   *   *

Phase Two: Find Yourself in Memories

Once you have allowed yourself to relax for a few days, review your life's journey to date by calling up memories of your past. This can be done in a linear or random fashion, depending on your personal preference. The purpose is to look for past experiences that give you clues as to what you really want to do and to identify those things you are doing because someone in your past placed a heavy expectation on you. There are several ways to go about calling up memories:

Look through your memorabilia and let your thoughts and emotions relive the experiences associated with particular items.

Glance through your old photo album and call up people, places and times that were significant to you.

Go to the public library and look at newspapers and magazines describing the significant historical events of your life.

If you have decided to return to your old stomping grounds for this experience, walk through your old neighborhood, your old school and other haunts, reflecting on the memories that arise from the experience.

Listen to music from various periods in your life to help bring up memories. For example, whenever I hear *Sgt. Pepper's Lonely Hearts Club Band*, I see myself waiting up until midnight on the day of its release, when radio stations could finally play the long-awaited album. I can see myself lying with my head actually underneath the old Magnavox console stereo with the volume as low as possible so as not to wake my parents. I remember the excitement of the new sounds, the feeling of amazement at the subtleties in the music, and the awakening desire to explore new musical possibilities for myself. Then I remember that summer, when you could always hear that record being played as you walked past houses and apartment complexes. Then I remember getting suspended from school for a couple of days for making out with my girlfriend in the junior high school locker area and going home that night to discover my dad had bought me *Sgt. Pepper* as a junior high graduation present...and on and on.

Keep a notebook with you to jot down your impressions. You will need them to complete the exercises on the following pages.

Tip:

If you can get in touch with smells during your journey through the past, you will be rewarded with rich memories. The olfactory sense has a powerful awakening effect. Since it is not yet technologically possible for people to keep scent albums, try walking through neighborhoods and natural settings at different hours of the day to enrich your experience. The smell of frying onions may remind you of coming home after school, the scent of moist earth may bring you back to a fond childhood memory, a whiff of a perfume or cologne may recall your first amorous experience.

*   *   *

Exercise: Finding Yourself in Memories

Go back through your notes and jot down the following information:

1.   What experiences in the past gave you a feeling of joy or excitement?
2.   What experiences in the past gave you pain or discomfort?
3.   Describe particularly memorable experiences where you wanted to do something but were told that you couldn't, you shouldn't or "if I were you I wouldn't." Whose tapes were going off in your head?
4.   Describe experiences where you tried to create something or do something that you were genuinely excited about but where an authority figure stopped you by either telling you that your work was no good or that it was a waste of time and energy.
5.   List recurring themes in your memories: people, places, things, events that seem to have kept popping up from time to time.

Review your previous answers before going on. Take a relaxation break if you'd like.

6.   Given what you've seen, what avenues have you shown a desire to explore?
7.   What talents do you have that are either unexplored (because someone stopped you from exploring those talents) or proven talents that you truly enjoy using?
8.   List what other people (parents, teachers, co-workers, spouses, friends, authority figures) have expected of you.
9.   Write down what you have expected of yourself, particularly those areas where you have been hard on yourself.
10.   Circle the areas of self-expectation that match the areas of other-expectation in the previous question. These are things you might consider letting go in the future. It might not be particularly easy to do so, because they may very well be the abilities you've used to build your current career!

11.　Summarize what you have learned about yourself so far, focusing on desires, dreams and potential:

Closing Phase Two

At this point, you are probably seriously exhausted. You may have touched some painful memories in the process of looking back. I cannot look back on my life without re-living the time when a woman who was very close to me was killed in a car accident. To this day, it's hard for me to look at her picture when I come across it in photo albums.

So, before going any further, put the book down and engage in a mindful activity. A mindful activity is anything that will completely occupy your mind and your senses. Select activities that will engage as many of your senses as possible. Movies are good because we can eat while we watch them, experiencing sight, sound, smell and taste in the process. Physical activity is a good possibility—hiking, shooting hoops, whatever. Loud restaurants (a Hard Rock Cafe, for example), music halls or dance clubs certainly qualify as multi-sensory experiences, as do most modern art museums.

The point is to get away from your exploration for awhile and enjoy yourself without thought or worry. Have fun!

*　　　　　*　　　　　*

Phase Three: Create Choices

Now that you've had a bit of time away from the issue at hand, you should be able to approach this next step in a more playful frame of mind. This is important because you are going to list possibilities for your future direction. When we are nervous, stressed or anxious, we tend to get evaluative and critical. If you do not feel relaxed, go back to the previous page and follow the instructions there.

Your choice of occupation is too important to limit yourself to a simple selection of A or B. It is equally important to move beyond the tendency to accept solutions that are "satisfactory" but may not be the best. We also have to move past both the expectations of others and the cultural myth that a person should be only one identifiable thing. We want to create several choices, not only to give you options for evaluation and selection, but to also express the full range of your capacity. Most people can do more than just the one thing that earns them the occupational label.

What is important in this exercise is to avoid "why nots". Although there may be several reasons "why not," most can be overcome through learning and a little help. If we are honest with ourselves, we will have to admit that most of the "why nots" are born in our own lack of confidence and fear of failure. At the other extreme, some very talented people even have a fear of success, worrying that it will compromise their talent or lead to an unwanted invasion of privacy. None of the self-generated reasons for avoiding responsibility to self are immutable laws of the universe, however. We can find ways to limit unpleasant side effects of our choices if we think carefully about those choices in advance. This can only be done if we give ourselves as many choices as possible, something that cannot be accomplished in a negative frame of mind.

It is equally vital that you avoid self-judgment, or more precisely, judgment regarding the possibilities you generate. If it is your personal desire to gain fame and status, say so, and don't feel guilty about it. If you have a secret desire to make your mark in the sex industry, don't let Puritan judgment get in your way. If what you really like to do is work with your hands, shut out the voices that describe such work as "menial." The voices in your head are not always yours but bits of tape you've collected from others over the years. Shut these out and don't judge yourself for your thoughts. If you repress possibilities at this stage, you will only experience stress later.

Tip:

If you've been away from the previous work for awhile, now is a good time to review what you've done so far. The desires of childhood are a good starting point for considering long forgotten possibilities. Reviewing those memories may yield some new directions.

When I was a kid, I wanted to go into politics. Given the current state of politics, that idea is no longer attractive to me. However, if I ask myself why, I find that I wanted to challenge unfairness in society. Now I have a new question, "How can I challenge unfairness in society without taking the political route?" This leads to new possibilities: I could start my own non-profit organization, I could write about it, I can get involved in children's groups to educate them about discrimination, and so on.

*   *   *

Exercise: Create Choices

1.   Take fifteen minutes and write down at least twenty avenues you think you might want to explore. Write them down even if you don't see how they can generate income or anything tangible. If you want to be a movie star, President of the United States, garbage collector or mixed media artist, write it down! Think of latent desires, talents and abilities you may want to realize.

        If you are stuck, complete the following phrases to add to your list:

        When I was a kid, I wanted to...

        When I was a teenager, I wanted to...

        When I got out of school, I wanted to...

2.   Go back through your list of avenues. As you read each one, listen for any tapes that play as you look at each option. If you don't hear any tapes but experience a flutter of excitement, then the choice is probably yours and you should circle it. If you hear voices telling you in one form or another that this is what you "should" be

doing, then it probably isn't yours. Cross it out. If you're getting a mixed message and you're not entirely sure what's going on, circle it. Some things that people expect of us may be things we want to do; the desire has been spoiled over the years by the unpleasant undertone of expectation.

3.   Write down the remaining avenues below. If you do not have at least ten, go back to the previous section and generate new possibilities.

4.   Now take the each avenue and describe the current abilities and talents you possess that can be applied to it:

Avenue   *Current Abilities/Talents*

       *   *   *

Phase Four: Define Purposes

Once you have mapped out the avenues available to you, it is a good idea to clarify the purposes behind each choice.

Why? There are several good reasons. First of all, there are many ways to achieve a particular purpose. By spelling out the broader intention behind your choice, you leave yourself open to other options, whether those options exist in the present or are opportunities that may manifest themselves in the future. Second, by defining your purposes you give yourself a sense of clarity that acts as a filter through which you can assess the various options that will come your way once you choose your directions. Third, writing down the purposes for each possible choice allows you to look for themes and connections that can give you an even wider outlook on what you want to do.

As before, don't be ashamed of your underlying purposes. This is the time to be honest with yourself about your true motivations. If you want to follow a certain path because you believe it will improve your love life or because it will make you a lot of money, don't judge yourself for it. We will look at false motivations in the next section and clean things up there. For now, simply look at your motivations and forgive yourself for being human.

There is, of course, another side to shame regarding purposes. Some people are embarrassed about expressing higher-level purposes such as wanting to change society or make the world safer for children. They think that higher-level purposes might sound a bit pompous. Or they might think that they would rather start with something less risky to forestall the possibility of failure. Nonsense! Again, the fundamental value behind all self-responsibility is "to thine own self be true," and if you repress any purpose, be it small or grand, you are not being responsible to yourself. In this exercise, just go for it.

The process we will follow is simple and direct: for each potential avenue of exploration, write your purpose in a single sentence, ask yourself why you want to achieve that and then consider alternative avenues that can get you there.

Tip:

It is critical to dig deep to uncover all underlying purposes. Let's say I wanted to be a movie director and I listed as a purpose, "I want to be able to combine the efforts of different artistic disciplines into a unified whole." I might look at that purpose and list an alternative like "museum curator," which certainly fits the bill. At that point, I might feel a bit of disappointment at that possibility, because I also want a bit of fame and notoriety, which does not come often to curators. Therefore, my purpose is really "I want to be able to combine the efforts of different artistic disciplines into a unified whole to produce successful movies that will garner some public attention for me." Now I'm being totally honest with myself and my purpose is clearer (and becoming a curator is probably out unless there's a major shift in our culture's values).

*   *   *

Exercise: Define Purposes

1.   For each avenue you listed in the previous exercise, write down the
     following answers (copy this page as often as necessary to cover all
     listed avenues).
     Why do I want to do this? (Purpose)
     Look at your purpose and write down at least three alternative
     avenues for achieving that purpose. Circle the avenues that appeal
     to you.
2.   Compile a list of the avenues you still want to explore, including
     any new alternatives that came to you in the process of doing
     this exercise:

     *   *   *

Phase Five: Face the Challenges

There are three primary obstacles to achievement, assuming one has the
desire to achieve. The first is a lack of information and knowledge about
what it takes. The second is the challenge of gaining the help and cooperation of others. The last involves what I call "disaster movies".

Disaster movies are files of pictures we keep in our brains that are activated when we experience certain fears. Confronted with what we dread,
our brains then begin to roll a film showing us of the impending disaster
we face if we choose a certain course of action.

That the disaster movie is entirely the creation of our own fears escapes
us. We treat the disaster movie as objective proof of our folly in thinking
we could accomplish our goals.

There are five primary fears and associated disaster movies we
experience:

The fear of not being good enough. The disaster movie includes pictures
of looking stupid or foolish.

The fear of change. This film shows everything going to hell as the result of failing to maintain the safety of the status quo.

The fear of vulnerability. This disaster flick features intense scenes of embarrassment and humiliation as the result of dropping our façades.

The fear of disappointment. This is an avant-garde film showing repeated instances of the lead character (you) missing out on something and then running around like crazy to recover what has been lost.

The fear of success. This is a blockbuster which opens with scenes of crowning achievement followed by repeated instances of not being good enough, unwanted change, public embarrassment and ultimate disappointment. It is motivated primarily by the fear of the increased expectations that accompany success.

After identifying what we do not know and who might be able to help us move in our intended directions, we will take a look at the disaster movies that play in our personal theaters during times of decision.

Tip:

Identifying what you need to know and who might be able to help you are relatively simple assignments. It is a simple matter of admitting what you do not know or have and then learning how to close the gaps.

Disaster movies are more of a challenge. They impact your entire life and may be called up in numerous and diverse circumstances. Grounded in basic fears that are part of our personality, they serve as filters through which we misinterpret the world. While you may have a very specific fear associated with a proposed course of action, the fears underlying disaster movies have the potential of distracting you from any direction you want to take. Be prepared that overcoming disaster movies will be a lifelong challenge.

*   *   *

Exercise: Face the Challenges

1. For each of the avenues you want to explore, list everything you don't know or feel you need to know about them. It is perfectly fine to create a list in the form of questions, because self-knowledge has more to do with admitting what you don't know than what you do know. Don't be embarrassed by your ignorance about a certain subject—learning is a critical component of self-responsibility.

   Avenue:

   Questions/Missing Information:

2. There are very few things in life that are accomplished by ourselves. Despite the star mentality that elevates individuals rather than groups into positions of prominence, all human accomplishments are the result of group effort. Implementing this step requires preparation, for you will not gain help and cooperation without effective communication skills. We will deal with those skills in the section on responsibility to others. For now, all you need to do is identify the people and organizations who may have knowledge, information or resources to help you with each of your possible avenues.

   Avenue:

   Potential Resources:

Bonus Tip

   A great place your search for resources to start is the Internet. Use your favorite search engine and type in words like "career," "change," "transition" and the like for organizations in those fields (of course, you may have to be persistent if your search results show 212,456 different keyword listings).

3. To identify which disaster movies are playing at your psychological theater, think about experiences you've had when you've

reacted defensively or out of all proportion to the reality of the situation. Check which apply to you (and yes, you may screen different disaster movies at different times, depending on your mood).

___If you've ever felt sorry for yourself and let everyone around you know it so you can get some validation, or if you have frozen solid when you have made a mistake, you have a *fear of not being good enough.*

___If you have ever persisted in unreasonable stubbornness in the face of a new situation, or have found yourself doing the same old thing even when there is clear evidence that your approach is likely to fail, you probably *fear change* more than is good for you.

___If you have ever displayed a streak of arrogance, particularly in situations where you've reduced a perceived attacker to crushed ice with a blast of cold sarcasm, you will have to admit that your show of strength is really a cover for your *fear of being vulnerable.*

___If you have ever exploded at the people around you at the slightest indication that they were not living up to your expectations, or beat yourself up when you failed to meet your own expectations, you are living with a constant *fear of disappointment.*

___If you repeatedly procrastinate when you have a clear opportunity to do the very thing you've said you've wanted to do, you could be suffering from a *fear of success.*

*   *   *

Trying to stop your disaster movies from playing is never easy. The source of the fears that run the movies is often a significant negative experience that occurred in childhood or adolescence. This makes it difficult to identify the source with any certainty. Furthermore, these movies are so embedded in our personalities that they may be things we will always have to live with to some degree. However, there are things we can do to minimize their impact on the choices we make and on the innocent people who happen to stumble onto our sets:

When you sense that the film is starting to play again, you will experience a welling of anxiety, anger, frustration or even panic. Learn the signals that tell you the film is about to begin.

Unless you're lucky enough to have a good friend nearby when the movie begins and unless you have the presence of mind to say to that friend, "I'm scared," it is probably best to avoid others while the film is rolling. Go for a walk, put on your Walkman, immerse yourself in video games, get some exercise. Caution: do not completely isolate yourself. Leave a door open or let people know where to reach you, as in, "I have to leave now to work something out but I'll be down the street if you need me."

Avoid alcohol, drugs or any other stimulant while you are in fear. These substances tend to cause the movie to play in a recurring loop.

Keep a log of the incidents that trigger a disaster movie and look for patterns. Identifying a consistent pattern can help you overcome a fear because patterns help explain things and understanding increases courage.

Forgive yourself for having a bad experience and apologize to anyone you may have hurt in the process.

A Note on Special Challenges

Some of you may have other challenges that go beyond fear, a lack of information or gaining allies. There are people who for various reasons experience prejudice or exceptional difficulties in the course of their lives. This can happen to people with disabilities, to women, to gays, to minorities, to senior citizens, to young people and even to white males in certain circumstances. Cultural myths notwithstanding, beautiful women are often handicapped both by the inaccurate but persistent stereotype that beauty does not go with brains and by the simple fact that they get more attention than the less beautiful, which can be as annoying as it is validating. Some people have regional accents or even English language barriers that others might interpret as evidence of low intelligence. In the United States, where money often speaks with authority, being poor is definitely an obstacle in certain enterprises. If you are "different" or do not fit the cultural expectation for a person in a particular field, you are going to have to face the fact that it will be tougher for you to do what you want to do.

It is easy for people facing these challenges to "play victim," because it is a culturally-sanctioned method of avoiding responsibility. While victimization is sometimes real, seeking permanent refuge in it is no way to achieve what you want to achieve. The best way to conquer resistance is to show the ignorant that you are capable.

In every field of endeavor, there are people who managed to overcome prejudice and perceived limitations to achieve great things. Many of them then used their new position of power to continue the cultural education process begun by their own success. While adopting someone as your "role model" is a questionable activity (you need to set your own unique course), studying the lives of those who have been successful in overcoming obstacles can be very enlightening.

Consider also the possibility that what you perceive as a weakness could be turned into an advantage for you. For example, people who are "different" do stand out from the crowd. Use your difference to expand awareness of the existence human capability in all shapes and sizes.

*   *   *

Exercises for Special Challenges

1. List any special challenges you face and name at least three people who have overcome those circumstances to achieve success in their field:

2. Consider ways in which you might turn your difference into an advantage for you, but avoid any actions you feel would compromise your values and integrity.

*   *   *

Summary of Progress

Now is a good time to summarize where you've come so far. Fill out one of these pages for each avenue on your list:

Avenue:

Capabilities/Talents:

Why I Want to Do This:

Other Options Available:

Obstacles:

> Things I need to learn:
> People I need to contact:
> Disaster movies I need to avoid:
> Special challenges:

*   *   *

Step Six: Planning for Balance

You've come a long way to get to this point. The next phase is easy.

You now have a list of at least ten avenues to explore, maybe more. Just as some streets look more inviting than others in a casual stroll around town, some avenues are going to have more of an emotional appeal to you than the rest. You will look at some and be infused with intensity; you will look at others and a little smile may cross your lips. There are some avenues you may not feel you're ready to walk, and there are others you can't wait to explore.

All of the avenues you have selected have a place in your life, if not now, then later. Human beings are capable of far more than just one thing, and this is your chance to organize those activities dearest to you into a structure that will keep them in the forefront of your busy life.

You will now classify the avenues into four areas: work, exploration, relaxation and play. The work avenues are those choices that fill you with passion and energy; you want to devote a lot of time to these activities because they are important to you and present a meaningful challenge. The exploration avenues are peripheral areas where you want to keep your hand in and learn more about them but do not want to make a commitment to a full-scale involvement at present. Relaxation avenues give you the opportunity to restore yourself. The play avenues are those activities that are fun for you. There may be some crossover between the avenues. After all, who says work cannot be fun? Who says work has to be stressful?

For example, my work areas include teaching, writing, facilitation and a little graphic design. They are all activities where I feel very purposeful and can imagine new possibilities. My exploration areas are acting, foreign affairs, architecture and painting. I am exploring those areas both for new work possibilities and as sources of ideas that I can transfer to my current work. Relaxation for me includes bubble baths and taking drives, both of which aid me enormously in my work. My play activities include music, basketball, attending arts and sporting events, and (blush) romance. These things help keep me grounded so I can approach work with focus.

You should end the exercise with at least three avenues classified in each of the four categories. Balance is critical, for we can become too consumed with our work, rendered incapable of action if we spend all our time exploring and feel completely empty if all we do is relax and play.

Tip:

How you classify things is up to you and a lot will depend on your gut feel. For example, basketball is one of my avenues. Being five feet six inches tall is a major obstacle to making that my work (not to mention a certain lack of talent at the free throw line). However, I can look to Muggsy Bogues and Spud Webb as examples of short men who overcame that obstacle to become NBA stars and try to follow in their equally tiny footsteps. Still, even though I know it's possible, I really don't want to put the effort into something that I perceive as involving too much sacrifice. In the end, I'm perfectly satisfied with the pick up games I play with my sons and will be content to leave Michael Jordan's legend unchallenged. Basketball therefore fits into the "play" category.

*   *   *

Exercise: Planning for Balance

Classify the avenues you've listed into work, exploration, relaxation or play:

WORK: *EXPLORATION:*   *RELAXATION:*   *PLAY:*

*   *   *

Phase Seven: Sacrifices

While you may want to rush off right now and begin leading your perfectly balanced existence, it is probably best to temper your enthusiasm with a small dose of reality. Yes, there's a real world back home, with real people and those annoying obligations.

There is a strong likelihood that you have obligations that have nothing to do with anything you have decided you want to do. You hate gardening with a passion, but you just bought a house and have stubbornly refused to pay for a gardener because of anxiety about your ever-mounting debt. You have a partner that you really don't get along with but you feel it's better than being alone. Perhaps you have made promises to other people and have created commitments you no longer want to keep. And you may be thinking goddamn it, why did I have to buy that new car last year? I need the money for video production equipment!

The problem with becoming self-responsible is that you do have to make sacrifices and those sacrifices often mean having to go back to other people to explain things. From your perspective, many of the sacrifices will be willing sacrifices, but you are not so sure that others will feel the same way. After all, they are human beings, too, and they will be likely to play their own disaster movies when they get wind of your new direction.

It all comes back to choice. You cannot be a responsible person if you compromise yourself to the extent that you hardly exist; then again, it is your choice to be responsible or not. You don't have to be responsible just because this book says you should be. But if you choose to become self-responsible, it is a change, and any change in you is going to unnerve those who are comfortable and content with predictable old you. You can minimize the pain of making the transition and the awkwardness of the situations you will face, but you cannot avoid it entirely, for you cannot control the choices of other human beings.

The exercises in this section prepare you to look at what it's going to take for you to pursue your avenues, the sacrifices will you have to endure, the obligations you might want to dissolve and the commitments you want to make to a new direction.

Tip:

There are a few people who will support you unconditionally. Talk to these people. Explain your problems, challenges and planned sacrifices. Ask them to help you think things through. In a time of personal change, people who unconditionally love you are your greatest source of support.

For those of you unfortunate enough to be surrounded by people who do not want you to change, try not to activate their underlying fears by softening your message or by trying to position it to show how what you're doing is in their best interests. When we play games like this, we are motivated by the fear of their reaction, and one of the truisms of communication is that if we communicate out of fear, we will get fear in return. Be direct, speak for yourself only, and listen carefully to their responses without becoming defensive.

*   *   *

Exercise: Sacrifices

For each avenue, answer the following questions.

Avenue:

Purpose:

What's it going to take in terms of...

      Money:

      Other Resources:

      Education:

      Time:

      People:

What sacrifices am I willing to make to pull this off:

      Money:

      Other Resources:

      Time (unnecessary activities I can give up):

      People:

What obligations do I currently have that may get in the way of achieving my purpose and how can I get rid of them, settle them or rearrange them to help me out?

Obligations: *Options:*

Once you share your decisions with others, you may find they begin rolling their own disaster movies and stop hearing what you have to say. To minimize the possibility of this occurring, think about the hot buttons of each person you need to approach. Identify the hot buttons and then return to the page describing disaster movies to correlate their reactions with a particular movie.

People: *Hot Buttons:*   *Disaster Movies:*

     *   *   *

Here are some tips on how to avoid triggering particular disaster movies. The most important preventive measure, however, is to do all you can to make sure you don't show your own disaster movie during the discussion:

Fear of not being good enough: Stress your confidence in the person's ability to help you through this crisis. This stops them from worrying about their own supposed inadequacy by channeling their energies into assistance.

Fear of change: Listen patiently to their concerns and fears. Stress the need for mutual help and give lots of hugs to reduce the likelihood of withdrawal.

Fear of being vulnerable: Do not allow yourself to become defensive when the arrows of arrogance start flying. Do not point out their fear of vulnerability either, for that will only cause them to aim for your heart. Instead, show your own vulnerability by asking for help, guidance and understanding.

Fear of disappointment: Let them run through the entire set of lost opportunities and then answer the objections calmly and rationally one by one. Try to show them that if opportunities have been lost, better opportunities have taken their place.

Fear of success: This will only arise if you are proposing a collaborative effort. If it does come up, no strategy is necessary. Talk about the risks and rewards of your proposed directions.

*   *   *

Phase Eight: Commitments

Now it is time to translate your work into a plan of action. This will not be your typical plan of action because we are going to build in a little forgiveness.

The first thing I am going to tell you *not* to do is set any fixed goals. This advice contradicts every other self-help book on the market. The reason why I advise against it at this stage is because frankly, you don't know what you're doing! Things may turn out to be harder (or easier) than you thought they would be and you certainly don't need to bear the guilt of a failed goal along with everything else you're trying to do.

Instead, look at yourself in the mirror every day and ask if you're being true to yourself. If you look real hard, that will keep you honest.

When all is said and done, you are the one that has to live with yourself. By stating a specific goal to others, you are setting up a system of having other people hold you accountable. The problem with such a system is that it transforms your pure desires into their contaminated expectations. This only confuses the issue and makes the work much less satisfying than it would be if pursued voluntarily. It's a major trap for those with a profound fear of disappointment, for when others are expecting great things out of you, it is likely you will feel too pressured to produce.

Only control freaks (primarily people with a fear of vulnerability) would even envision a system (similar to those used in most American corporations) of assigning the responsibility for holding a person accountable to someone other than the person truly responsible. In corporations, they feel the need to control people because many people don't really want to do what they're doing. Here you are doing what you want to be doing and you need only that occasional look in the mirror to monitor your progress. The control comes from within and from the simple fact that you have responsibilities, not necessarily obligations to others (as discussed in the next chapter).

What you are going to do in this section is set your directions, not your final destinations. You're going to start your journey with the openness of an explorer on uncharted seas. You have some things you want to see and on the way you may decide to set out for a particular destination. But your overall strategy is fixed to your purpose, not the details. This will allow you to stay open to learning and new information, a critical component in achieving self-responsibility.

When I say to avoid goal setting, I do not mean losing touch with your purposes. Your purposes should be close to you. You should read them weekly and change them as you gain more knowledge and strength.

However, you do not want to catch the American disease of scheduling and planning everything in one's life. When you plan your time to excess, you may miss more relevant opportunities because you create an obligation to stick to Plan A. Planning your time also limits your ability to improvise, and in a world of high-speed change, the ability to improvise is vital. If you really need to set a time-bound activity goal, like taking a class in ceramics in the fall quarter for three nights a week after work, consider the consequences and potential losses as well as the potential gains.

*   *   *

Exercise: Commitments

1.   When I get back into my day-to-day existence, these are the things that are going to be different:
        These are the sacrifices I'm going to make:
        These are the things I'm going to learn more about:
        These are the people I need to talk to or who may be able to help me:
        I am committed to exploring these avenues and achieving these purposes:
        Avenue   *Purpose*

Congratulations!

By engaging in self-reflection and by committing to an integrated structure of self-maintenance, self-development and self-forgiveness, you are now ready to move forward and make more conscious choices about what you're doing in your life, particularly in the work you do. You now have the power to make choices without settling for the default choice.

Please note that I did not say that you now will experience unlimited joy and happiness. I have not even hinted at the possibility that you will now "gain control of your life." You have a better understanding of yourself and are certainly more grounded as the result of going through this process. However, happiness depends on a number of variables, and trying to establish control over one's life not only limits possibilities but begins with an intellectual error. That error involves the simple fact that you are not alone and that other people will in fact impact your life, whether you want them to or not.

We are now ready for a discussion of the two aspects of responsibility beyond the self, your responsibility to others and your responsibility to the communities you choose to serve.

RESPONSIBILITY TO OTHERS

Once we have chosen the avenues we want to investigate, we inevitably run up against the sometimes unfortunate existence of other human beings.

These are members of a highly problematic species. They often have other ideas and ways of doing things that do not fit with the way we think things should be done. Communication with these beings is frequently difficult, as most of them do not listen and only a few can express themselves with any clarity. Human beings are often cold, indifferent and aggressive, turning to violence either in an attempt to solve problems or just for the hell of it. Some humans cooperate more effectively with other species such as canines and whales than they do with their own kind, and for good reason. None of the other species on the planet can match the capacity of the human race for senseless physical and psychological cruelty to other life forms, including its offspring. Although nature presents us with endless puzzles and mysteries in many forms, nothing in the natural world can compete with the puzzles and mysteries created by the human animal. Despite extensive efforts in the arts and sciences to figure out this complex race, the capacity of human beings to deceive themselves and others seems forever capable of blocking any reliable understanding. Living with and working with other human beings is a curse we have to bear up to our dying breath, when hopefully we will be rid of them, their whiny demands for more attention and their petty complaints about everything under the sun.

There is, of course, an alternative view.

In another version of the story, humans are creators of vast stores of knowledge that they use for the betterment of themselves and other species sharing the planet. Human beings are capable of astonishing acts of tenderness and kindness, of works of penetrating insight and intelligence, of extraordinary sacrifices for the good of their fellows. No other species has come together in the face of enormous odds to create civilizations and the great works of art and commerce that define those civilizations. No experience in the known universe can match the power of giving and receiving unconditional human love, which explains why human beings spend a significant amount of their waking hours in pursuit of friendship and romance. This is a race of high ideals, of strenuous effort, of limitless curiosity and an insatiable desire to push the limits of mind, body and spirit. From this race comes such noble and gifted souls as Stephen Hawking, Mother Theresa, Emily Dickinson, Martin Luther King and William Shakespeare; from this race also comes millions of simple and anonymous people who live the parable of the Good Samaritan by performing daily acts of kindness. This is a species that takes special care of its children, its parents often sacrificing their own desires for the hope of a better future for their offspring.

Whichever view you hold of the human race, the important point is that you are going to have to deal with people as you pursue your goals. This requires effort, understanding and more than a little skill. There is no guarantee that your interactions with other people will give you the results you want, even if you communicate with precision and sensitivity. However, while you may never get through to a psychopath bent on your destruction, you can get through to most people, although it frequently takes some doing.

You can increase your chances of success by being responsible to others and acting accordingly. Change may begin with the individual but it only begins to thrive when others support and sustain it.

The Social Context

As mentioned previously, we live in a society that is extremely confused about responsibility. There is a persistent "the devil made me do it" urge in many of our fellow citizens that causes them to blame their own evil acts or shortcomings on others. Blame has been legitimized in organizations, in the media (providing the content of most news programs), in relationships, in the constant pattern of self-justification that seems to contaminate most of our conversations. If something goes wrong "someone" must "be responsible," and because we grant people the inalienable right to confuse the issue (a trait inherited from our political leaders), the search for the culprits leads to some intellectual gymnastics. Therefore, corporations become responsible for the violent acts of their employees because "they should have known," responsible for fluctuations in stock prices because "they should have known," and for simple accidents involving their products because "they should have known." These attempts to hold corporations accountable often have very little to do with responsibility. Responsibility is simply the word conjured up to disguise the underlying profit motive of the "poor victim," and the target of the lawsuit is rarely the debt-ridden individual perpetrator but the deep pockets of the corporation.

Even though corporations, governments and other institutions sometimes act as if they are responsible for the people they employ, treating employees as idiots incapable of making intelligent choices, that does not mean they are to blame for the actions of the people who work there. If the leader of a corporation lies to the stockholders so they cannot make intelligent decisions about what to do with the money, then that leader should explain him or herself, but to say that the corporation is "responsible" is ludicrous. Inanimate abstract creations like "corporations" or "organizations" or "governments" cannot experience responsibility. Only individual human beings with names and faces can experience responsibility.

One of my favorite leaders in organizational life has a peculiar policy. He refuses to accept a complaint from an employee that blames "them" or "that department" or any other abstraction. "Who? Who? Who told you that? Who said it couldn't be done? Have you talked to that person and tried to work things out?" He refuses to accept the tendency of people to depersonalize situations, since that tactic only makes it easier for the sniper to take potshots. He understands that at the root of all human problems you will find people, not impersonal systems. He also understands that people can solve problems whereas inanimate objects are comparatively ineffective.

Remember, we do not equate responsibility with blame in this book. The leader mentioned above understands that responsibility is partially an act of identifying who might be available to help. If responsibility were instead treated as a learning experience rather than an opportunity to attack or a chance to exploit a large bank account, not only would we put the legal profession out of business, but we might become capable of resolving problems together.

Prepositional Clarification

We need to clarify is a crucial preposition. When we say "responsible *to* others," we do not mean "responsible *for* others."

Once a person reaches adulthood (and, please, let's not get into that silly legal debate about how old someone has to be before we can rightfully nail them for something), he or she is generally capable of making their own choices. No one else is responsible for those choices. No one. Not God, not heavy metal, not the corporation, not the influence of television violence, not bad parents. The influences of any human or superhuman force can be overcome by a person who chooses to do so. It may take help from a professional or a friend, but every functional person has choices. They can use their experience as an excuse or try to rise above it.

This does not mean, however, that we simply wipe our hands of any potential association with the acts of other people. We are responsible to those people by nature of the fact that we share the human experience. "We are all in this together" is the true motto of the human race, and no one can effectively escape that fact, even the most anti-social person on the planet. "I am he as you are he as you are me and we are all together" finally begins to make sense.

Things get complicated when we change the preposition and instead of being responsible *to* someone, we try to become responsible *for* someone. We try to limit their choices. We try to tell them what they should do. We try to control them through direct threat or subtle manipulation. We give them advice that only serves to publicize our own preferences instead of really helping someone in need. And above all, we burden others, from parents to leaders to children to lovers, with expectations aplenty.

Just as "to thine own self be true" is the motto of self-responsibility, "do unto others as you would have them do unto you" is the motto of responsibility to others. The problem is that people throughout history have voiced agreement with the sentiments contained in the Golden Rule but have rarely taken the time to figure out how to implement the philosophy in their daily activities. Although we are not going to pretend to have the wisdom of Christ and Confucius at our disposal, we can identify several actions people can take to become more responsible to others, thus creating relationships through which people can face life together.

The six basic actions of responsibility to others are:
Seek the true self
Respect choices
Offer assistance with choices
Communicate truth
Define your parameters
Learn forgiveness

Seek the True Self

Your first and primary responsibility to another human being is to find out who they are.

This does not mean sticking your nose into their private lives or invading their space. If they choose to present very little of themselves to you, that's their business. It isn't so much what we know or don't know about people that makes the crucial difference in understanding them. What blocks our understanding of others is our expectations of how they should act.

We all have a series of "shoulds" lurking about in our minds for nearly every conceivable role we might come across in the course of our existence. When people fail to live up to our "shoulds," we can be ruthless. This is most obvious in our attitudes towards public figures, to whom we have denied the right to be human. Athletes should behave a certain way, so we resent people like Dennis Rodman. Royalty shouldn't go around showing their breasts, so Sarah Ferguson lost points for that. Leaders should be morally upright and impeccably fair, so we run them up the flagpole when they make mistakes. Parents are always complaining that their children are not living up to their potential, although in most cases that potential was defined by the parents' need for status and not by the child's interests or abilities. Often we have more shoulds in intimate relationships than anywhere else, as evidenced by the ability to dismiss potential partners for such insignificant defects as poor clothing choices or small bank accounts.

Shoulds are invariably unfair because there is no person on the planet capable of being the ultimate judge about how a person should act. Our personal tastes render us completely incapable of judging the personal preferences of others. As long as those actions result in no harm to another human being (and this means without the devil-made-me-do-it legal twisting of the meaning of "harm"), we are on very shaky ground when we try to stop those actions. We would certainly want other people to do the same to us, and "judge as ye not be judged" is as true as the Golden Rule.

Therefore, the first step in being responsible to others is to eliminate the shoulds from your psyche. This is not easy, because most people do not believe they have them. Try the following exercise to uncover your personal shoulds:

*   *   *

Exercise: Identifying Expectations of Others, Part 1:

Simply fill in the blanks to begin discovering the shoulds you may impose on others:

A man should be…
A woman should be…
Children should be…
My children should be…
Teachers should be…
Leaders should be…
My co-workers should be…
Public figures should be…
(Your choice) should be…
(Your choice) should be…

*   *   *

Exercise: Identifying Expectations of Others, Part 2:

Your "should bes" require more explanation. You may know what they mean but others do not. Because expectations are grounded in unconscious assumptions, uncovering those assumptions is the key to developing authentic relationships.

Example:

Let's say you wrote "a man should be masculine". Ask yourself what masculine means in terms of what a man is supposed to do and not supposed to do to live up to your beliefs.

A man should be masculine. This means that a man should do these things: watch sports, go hunting, show their chest hair. This means that a man should not do these things: wear pink, show emotions, give in too easily.
Now you try it for each of your shoulds.

A man should be_____.
This means that a man should do these things:
This means that a man should not do these things:
A woman should be_____.
This means that a woman should do these things:
This means that a woman should not do these things:
Children should be_____.
This means that children should do these things:
This means that children should not do these things:
My children should be_____.
This means that my children should do these things:
This means that my children should not do these things:
Teachers should be_____.
This means that teachers should do these things:
This means that teachers should not do these things:
Leaders should be_____.
This means that leaders should do these things:
This means that leaders should not do these things:
My co-workers should be_____.
This means that my co-workers should do these things:
This means that my co-workers should not do these things:
Public figures should be_____.
This means that public figures should do these things:
This means that public figures should not do these things:
(Your choice)___should be_____.
This means that_____
should do these things:

This means that _____
should not do these things:
When you have completed the exercise, perform two additional steps:
1. Look for obvious examples of unfair or unreasonable expectations.
2. Where possible, share your expectations with others who fall under each category. Ask them what they think of your expectations and listen carefully.

Once you have exposed the expectations for what they are—personal preferences that have little relation to universal rules—you will become more conscious of your attempts to impose them on others.

*   *   *

Respect Choices

The hardest part of letting go of responsibility *for* others is learning to let others make their own choices.

Yes, even if you think those choices are stupid choices.

We are often motivated by good intentions in this regard. We don't want to see other people get hurt so we try to stop them from taking hopeless courses of action. We want to help children get through life with less damage than we did, so we work to prevent them from getting into the same kinds of scrapes we did when we were their ages. I would want to ground my sons for months if they even thought of doing some of the stupid things I did when I was young.

The problem has to do with how people learn. We learn the harder lessons through personal experience, not through lecture or example. We may gather all sorts of valuable information from books and literature but until we experience the literary analogy in action, we have only a dim understanding of what it really means. So although we don't want people to get hurt, sometimes the bruises are necessary for a person to really get it. Parents, of course, have to use their best judgment to determine how far one can allow a child to make choices, which is always a difficult decision. Still, even children have the capacity to make intelligent choices, and sometimes their choices turn out to be higher-quality selections than the parents would have made for them. After all, just because something did not work out for you does not mean it will not work for another.

We also need to factor human defiance into the equation. Trying to prevent people from making certain choices often leads people to choose the very thing we wanted them to reject. This is classically true for adolescents, but it is also true for employees who feel they are being excessively controlled and want to defy repressive authority. Even if mom or dad or the boss tell us that such-and-such is not a good idea, something inside us compels us to try it out for ourselves anyway. After all, mom and dad (and bosses) can make mistakes, too.

Usually we do not slam our fists on the relational table and demand that a person not do a certain thing. We're sneakier than that. Our preferred form of controlling others is "helpful advice," which manifests itself as telling a person what you would do if you were in their proverbial shoes. The problem is that in giving advice, we are trying to accept responsibility for another person, which is invariably a mistake. Even when people are asking for advice, it is still unwise to give it, for all you wind up doing is supporting their avoidance of personal responsibility.

Sometimes the choices others make frighten us. We worry about how we will look, how things will appear to the outside world or what will happen to us as the result of this choice. Disaster movies begin to play in our heads. However, it is fundamentally unfair to stop another person from acting because that person has activated a fear for which we are responsible. The ultimate act of responsibility to others may be overcoming our fears to permit others freedom of action. One way to work through the fear is to identify our choices in the situation, which helps us move away from paralysis and into action.

In general, then, trying to stop people from making choices we do not like is a counterproductive activity. About the only thing it achieves is resentment from the person you are trying to control. It also provides the recipient with a easily accessible scapegoat in case things go wrong. You may not like their choices, and you certainly have the right to choose your own course in relation to their choice, but the decision is ultimately theirs.

*   *   *

Exercise: Letting Go of Responsibility for Others

Write down at least three experiences where you have tried to block the choices of others. Look at your personal and working relationships for experiences of this kind. Use the format below to help you identify your patterns of controlling others (see the example on the following page):

When (person) _____hose to

(action)_____

I (response)_____

I did this because I was afraid that...

_____

I do not have to be afraid because I have these choices:

_____

Example: Letting Go of Responsibility for Others

When (person) *my significant other* chose to (action) *go back to school at night* I (response) *blew up at her and told her that she didn't care about my needs.*

I did this because *I was afraid that she might meet someone else at school who was more interesting and that we would no longer have quality time together.*

I do not have to be afraid because I have these choices:

I can help her with her schoolwork.

I can take a few classes myself.
I can identify the sources of my insecurity and work on them.

*   *   *

Offer Assistance with Choices

Backing off the Dear Abby role does not mean abandoning another person to the winds of fate. There are things you can do that are truly helpful and keep your responsibility channels clear.

We face dozens of choices every day. We choose what we wear, what we eat, what route we're going to take to work, whether or not we can really afford to eat that doughnut, what to do about various work-related problems, whom to have dinner with and so on. Most of those choices are automatic, determined by simple logic or habit.

However, everyone faces more difficult choices from time to time. The nature of difficult choices is that they often appear in the form of contradictory or vague information, forcing our values and beliefs into conflict with each other, testing our intellect and emotional strength. Some of the difficult situations I have experienced include learning to cope with alcoholics, facing the fact that someone betrayed my trust, and having to choose between financial reward and personal fulfillment. In every difficult situation I have faced, my natural tendency has been to turn inward, to blame myself for the problem, to adopt Emerson's notion of self-reliance to the extreme and try to handle things myself.

This was always a mistake. I had people around me who were willing to help and I refused to acknowledge it. Had I taken advantage of their assistance, I might not have lost so much sleep or struggled so hopelessly with my problems.

I say these people were willing to help because they did not offer advice, but simply made themselves available to talk. Whenever I finally broke out of my stubborn refusal to accept assistance, I always found their aid valuable. Different friends possessed different strengths and perspectives that could be brought to bear on my problem.

We need to help people through their choices, not just stand idly by and let them suffer. Compassion is an essential part of our responsibility to others. While we must always discipline our compassion with our responsibility to ourselves, that does not give us an excuse to withdraw from human contact. While there are people in the world who cynically exploit human compassion, we can learn to temper our compassion with the wisdom of experience without hiding behind defensive fortifications. We can indeed help others without hurting ourselves.

To offer assistance to others, then...

Tell the person in need that you are available to help them think, feel and choose for themselves, not to give advice. You may need to repeat this offer several times before the person accepts it, depending upon the extent of their pride. Then be sure to make yourself available! There is nothing worse than offering help without the commitment to be there when it is needed.

Help them identify the known facts surrounding the situation. Feel free to state facts that they may have ignored or may not be aware of. When people are feeling stressed, they have a hard time taking in information.

Allow them to freely express their feelings about the matter and listen carefully without judging those feelings as appropriate or inappropriate. Permit them to tell you what they think it all means, but instead of correcting what you think are misinterpretations, offer alternative suggestions that could explain the situation.

Help them consider possible actions they can take in response to the situation. Throw out options they may not have considered, but keep encouraging them to express options themselves. You may have to get past the "there's nothing I can do" script, but persevere until you think you have done all you can. You can use the "what would happen if" question several times to create options. Make sure their answers to "what would happen if" questions do reflect the real set of circumstances.

Communicate Truth

It may sound obvious to tell people to communicate truthfully with each other. After all, it wouldn't make any sense to encourage people to lie, would it?

While I have known one or two pathological fibbers in my time, most people do not tell out-and-out lies. They bend the truth in other ways. They hint at what they need rather than saying it directly. They use sarcasm to express dissatisfaction with another person's actions rather than simply describing what it is they are unhappy about. Most often, people simply shut their mouths and avoid saying anything altogether, since they have learned through their working experiences that it's better to be silent than dead.

This is not the book to teach you how to communicate effectively. For specific communication skills, I refer you to that all-time classic, *Messages: The Communication Book* by McKay, Davis and Fanning. That book contains all the basic skills to assist you in improving your clarity in both listening and expression, at home and on the job.

What I do want to emphasize is that what you communicate should have one primary quality: it must be honest. Honest communication reveals itself when a person is speaking for him or herself and no other. It is free of judgment but not free of emotion. Using the "Whole Message" process described in *Messages*, honest communication consists of four components: observations, thoughts, feelings and needs, which are in turn disciplined by the overriding considerations of being direct, supportive, clear, immediate and truthful.

The degree of openness you choose to exercise in your communication is up to you. Honesty and openness are not the same thing. You may be quite honest without being open (and vice versa). The boundaries of openness are determined by the context in which you are communicating. Being open about a problem you see in the engineering design specs is a responsible action in the workplace. Being open in the workplace about your recreational drug use is suicidal. You need to share what is relevant to other people so they can make effective choices. You do not have to divulge private matters (unless you are in the context of an intimate relationship and are willing to do so).

Remember that what is relevant in the context of the organization is restricted by various rules, norms and laws. If you are an extremely open person with a strong value of openness, you may want to consider options other than Corporate America or any other regulated workplace in your search for income.

The important point is that you owe it to other people, based on the good old Golden Rule, to tell them the whole truth and nothing but the truth when the matter directly affects them. Without accurate information, people cannot make intelligent decisions.

Defining Your Parameters

One important aspect of communicating the truth has to do with your personal limits. Allowing people to make choices is not the same as giving insensitive people license to trample all over you and your rights. It is not only acceptable but it is essential to express your parameters to other people very, very clearly.

Your parameters are your limitations as to how far you can go with another person in a given situation. Expressing them completes the circle you began by seeking the other's true self. This is where you share parts of who you are, particularly what you are willing to tolerate and what you cannot.

The reason this is so important is people have different levels of tolerance depending on the circumstances. I learned this most poignantly when I did back to back training sessions in distinct geographical areas. The first group was a group from New York City. When I did an exercise that called on people to identify their most admired person, Donald Trump won hands down. As the class proceeded, I noticed that no one in the room could express a complete thought without using the words, "fuck" and "bullshit." They also had the remarkable ability to talk in the middle of lectures, videos and other training activities and still take in everything that was going on.

The following week I went to the Deep South. Jesus Christ crushed the competition for most admired person. The strongest language I heard used all week was "dang." They were eminently polite and shushed anyone who talked during a video. They were always on time, even after breaks and lunches.

The Southerners were not any more "well-behaved" than the New Yorkers. Their particular cultures had different definitions of what constitutes acceptable public behavior. The New Yorkers would have had a hard time putting up with Southerners telling them to shush. The Southerners would have had a hard time listening to what they considered to be foul language.

Cultural differences are often the source of many misunderstandings, largely because we are so terribly ethnocentric in America. We have a hard time understanding why people are not like us. We forget that culture is not universal. We forget that culture is hardly a conscious experience; that people do not stop to explain what they are like, because they are busy just being who they are. We approach others based on a set of taken-for-granted assumptions we rarely question. In a culture as diverse as ours, though, we need to realize that our assumptions about the way things should be do not hold for everyone and make sure we communicate clearly what we find acceptable and what we do not.

It is important to do this without an air of judgment. If you are a non-smoker, telling someone who just lit up that you do not want to be around the smoke and you would prefer that the person smoked elsewhere is fine. You have just established your parameters clearly and succinctly. However, giving the same message in a sarcastic, judgmental or paranoid tone will hardly help the situation. "I can't believe there are people who still smoke!" you might say. Or, "How dare you foul my air?" These statements are judgmental and unlikely to promote cooperation. You have the right to describe your limits but you do not have the right to demean people in the process.

Therefore, if someone offends you or proposes something you think is risky, you have the responsibility to inform that person clearly and succinctly of your position. Most people do not do this in organizational life, which often results in disasters that could have been easily avoided. Even if a person may not want to hear it, you owe it to that person to let him or her know where you stand. If others are clear about your boundaries, it helps them become clearer about their choices.

Forgiveness

The final responsibility we have to others is to forgive them when they make mistakes or do us harm.

This is a difficult moral issue. We have swung entirely too far in the other direction, willing to string up every deviant bastard in sight. However, the culture of blame is wreaking havoc within our organizations, not only because of increased legal cost, but also in the millions of ideas that are lost because people have become terrified of making public mistakes and taking the heat for them.

Being far from enlightened myself, I know that there are certain things I could never forgive. If a person harmed either of my children, or my significant other, or any other person I love dearly, I would have a very hard time restraining myself from breaking every bone in the perpetrator's body. To take a life is unforgivable, as is forcible rape. I have a hard time feeling forgiveness when someone has used their physical power to harm another; it's just so animalistic and unfair. I also struggle with leaders who arrogantly abuse their power, and with employees who take advantage of the system and wind up hurting their friends and co-workers through selfish actions. I could probably forgive a person who did something that violated my principles or my trust if they showed remorse, but I really doubt my ability to forgive a murderer, a rapist or a child molester.

Then again, who suffers the most from withholding forgiveness? The unfeeling murderer who obliterated someone's choices doesn't care whether I forgive or not. Failing to forgive only winds up eating away at me and so I suffer by failing to let go of the bitterness I feel.

There are both religious and secular texts on the subject that explore the nature of forgiveness more deeply than we can in this book. Let us summarize this discussion as follows: your responsibility to others may not mean automatically forgiving those who directly or indirectly cause you harm. Whether you forgive someone is up to you and based on your own moral code. I will argue, though, that your responsibility to others is to take advantage of every opportunity for forgiveness that presents itself to you, of every situation where you will not have to compromise your values and violate your ultimate responsibility to yourself. This is particularly applicable to life in the workplace, where too many people are taking the heat for simply being human.

It can't be that hard to forgive the essential humanity that we all share.

RESPONSIBILITY TO COMMUNITY

Most human beings feel the need or desire to contribute to something beyond themselves. Part of this urge is no doubt grounded in our desire to escape death by achieving immortality via proxy. Perhaps some of it has to do with the genetic programming of primates, who generally tend to form communal units to promote the common defense and general welfare. Some people believe that we are essentially one and that on a soul level individual differences vanish into the reality of spiritual unity, although this is difficult to accept if you've ever watched your kindred spirits humiliate themselves as the television camera pans the crowd at any sporting event.

Whatever the cause behind our drive to pursue something greater than ourselves, and whether that something greater truly exists or is paradoxically created by our belief in it, the need for human beings to form communities is inescapable. On a macro level, we form societies based upon general agreements called laws that people more or less support with the idea that they will get a sense of order in return. On a micro level, families are created both by blood and life circumstances, forming a unit with an identity greater than the sum of its parts. People have a need to belong, and while this is sometimes taken to extremes, communities serve to satisfy a basic human need.

However, it is debatable whether communities can be responsible in the meaning we have attached to the word. While we can say that such-and-such community responded effectively to a disaster like a flood, that sort of statement is more of a generalization than an accurate description of what really happened. It is likely that a majority of the community sat on their behinds while a few of the more energetic members stuffed the sandbags into place. It is also questionable to assert that communities can make choices, for no matter how united a community may be, there is rarely perfect agreement between all the members. Without choice, the issue of responsibility is meaningless. Therefore, when we use the phrase "collective responsibility," we must acknowledge its inaccuracy and the fact that it is of lower quality than individual responsibility.

It is because the responsibility of a community is more concept than reality that individual commitment becomes the critical factor in sustaining a community. If members do not exercise their ability to respond effectively to situations facing the community, the community will die. The only thing that truly sustains a community is individual effort and commitment, and while rules and regulations can hold things together for a time, no community can survive for long without the investment of energy on the part of a significant number of its members.

Inclusion and Exclusion

Defining membership in a community has always been a tricky issue, as many communities tend to be exclusive instead of inclusive. The people who establish and sustain the community often set up barriers to keep the people who are "not-like-us" out. This is true for formal communities like the National Basketball Association (who keep low-talent people like me off the court) or for informal communities like teenagers-who-wear-cool-shoes. Sometimes the exclusion is arbitrary and laden with prejudice; in other situations, exclusion exists for valid reasons (the NBA would go out of business if its fans had to watch people like me at the free throw line every night).

Exclusion becomes a problem in two scenarios. The first occurs when the members of a community forget that they are part of a larger society. When this happens, they ignore their responsibilities to the greater community or even to the people the community is supposed to serve. Companies forget about their customers, the environment, and the economic impact of their presence on the local community. Sports teams ignore the wishes of their fans and either jack up ticket prices to form a more exclusive community or move to other locations. The people the community serves are often forgotten or treated as insignificant outsiders because they do not really "belong." The primary cause of this problem is the creation of exclusionary groups (the so-called "insiders") within the community itself. If organizations create internal territories and status hierarchies, decision-makers will be far more likely to adopt exclusionary tactics against the outside world because they learn to view others as threats.

The second scenario in which exclusion becomes a problem is when the exclusion is arbitrary or unfair. This is the most dangerous form of exclusion for it creates resentment and bitterness on the part of the excluded. Some strike back at the community who rejected them, while other outcasts form alternative communities to manifest the need to belong. Examples of the exclusion process abound even in our free and fair society. Because a majority of Americans feel their vote is completely meaningless, they have turned to the formation of special interest groups in order to be heard. Because throughout our history we have excluded minorities, women and non-heterosexuals from mainstream participation, we have vast numbers of groups working to protect their rights. This development is neither right nor wrong. It is simply a manifestation of the human need for community. People will seek out communities with intensity and when excluded from one, they will either create a new one or declare war on the old one.

An interesting mutation of the community-forming tendencies of human beings is the emergence of cyber-communities. People from all over the world are forming newsgroups and chat rooms with those who share common interests. While the quality of such interactions leaves something to be desired (if you've ever been in a chat room, you'll know what I mean), the fact that these groups have very few membership requirements while defying traditional filters such as age, race, gender and national boundary make them viable and attractive communities for many people. Of course, one has to be able to afford a personal computer or use the employer's system to log on to the Internet, so there are some exclusionary influences in operation. However, what cyber-communities demonstrate is not only the existence of the human need for bonding but also that people are looking outside traditional channels to manifest that need.

The primary community for most of us, however, is not the World Wide Web but that other "w," the workplace. Many people do not think of the workplace as a community, but as a regrettable financial arrangement where both parties use each other to get what they want. Executive decision-makers in American corporations have hardly shown much loyalty to their employees lately, but on the other hand, there are plenty of employees who have either screwed their employers or decided to check out, take up space and pick up a paycheck. The problem with such an arrangement is that it is not fair to anyone involved. The community (in this case, the company) becomes filled with members who are not willing to contribute, thereby limiting its ability to meet its goals. Disgruntled workers form smaller shadow communities whose sold purpose is to complain, not act. The individual employee cheats him or herself by stubbornly refusing to work to their potential. Without an ethic of shared responsibility, this no-win loop will never be broken. Furthermore, this ethic must be adopted by individual executives who refuse to hide behind the corporate mask as well as individual employees who refuse to wear the guise of victimization. A "corporation" can always downsize because an abstract entity has no humanity. A person playing victim has depersonalized himself or herself to achieve the same kind of separation from responsibility. Only individual human beings with a sense of responsibility to self, other and community can address the problem and end the dehumanizing practices of the workplace and in our other communities.

As mentioned before, there are four responsibilities involved in becoming responsible to a community: making the commitment, supporting the members, meeting obligations and quitting when it's time to quit. Let's review each in turn.

Making the Commitment

Commitment seems to be losing favor. We are unhappy about free agency in sports (unless you are an athlete) because it explodes the myth of loyalty to the team. More than half of all marriages end in divorce. Lifetime employment at a single company is a fading dream. The cyber-community reflects a new set of values in that all one has to do to leave the community is disconnect the modem. Communities and relationships now seem more a matter of convenience than commitment.

While convenience has its advantages, some level of continuity is required to succeed in any enterprise. People have to check each other out and get to know each other a little before they can work effectively together. Convenient and collapsible communities may give us a superficial buzz of involvement but one cannot experience the deeper satisfaction that comes with shared learning that occurs over a length of time and a breadth of experience.

However, there are very good reasons why commitments are not kept. Many commitments are born out of expectations as to what we should be doing, and unless a commitment is cemented by our desire to keep it, it is always a fragile thing. Other commitments are simply unfair; the reserve clauses that bound a player to a particular team denied the individual the opportunity to make choices. Excessive hype has a lot to do with broken commitments; we get all excited about the advertising associated with a community organization or club we would like to join and are often disappointed when we arrive at the first meeting and discover a bunch of status-hungry bores.

Therefore, rid yourself of the notion that all commitments must be kept and replace it with the preventive orientation that no commitment should be entered into unless one has carefully reviewed what it involves and the consequences of that involvement. Irresponsibility comes from entering commitments that we have not thoroughly checked out in advance, but have taken on because we were swayed by fear, marketing or unrealistic expectations.

Therefore, to properly review a potential commitment, ask yourself or the other parties involved the questions contained in the following list:

*　　　　　*　　　　　*

Reviewing Community Involvement, General

How much time and energy will it take to be a fully involved member of this community?

What expectations do the leaders of the community have of their members?

What is the purpose of this community?

What does this community do to support its members?

Whom does this community include and why?

Whom does this community exclude and why?

What specific opportunities exist for you to contribute to this community?

What do the other community members want or expect from you?

What other commitments come with membership in this community?

*　　　　　*　　　　　*

Reviewing Community Involvement: Workplace

If you are on a job interview, translate the above questions as suggested in the following list. Be sure you ask everyone the same questions to measure the reliability of the answers.

How much time and energy do you expect me to contribute if I want to be successful on this job?

What expectations do you have of your employees? (You can ask about specific concerns here such as policy, dress code, limits on private behavior, "professionalism," etc.)

What is the purpose of this organization? This workgroup?

What kind of support does this organization give its people? (Ask about specifics including training, technology, benefits and participation.)

What kind of people do you want working here?

What kind of people does you *not* want working here?

How do you see me contributing to this company? How do you see me making a difference?

Is it possible for me to interview with the people I will be working with? I want to ask them about their expectations of me.

What other commitments beyond an honest day's work do I need to make to achieve success here?

The message here is that you make a commitment, go in with your eyes open and you will have a much better chance of a positive relationship.

*　　　　　*　　　　　*

To aid you in obtaining a real understanding of commitment, Appendix 1 includes a general review of the major working arenas, from government to non-profits to the military to the arts. Review these listings for information about the assumptions dominating a particular working environment.

Once you choose an arena, find an organization and make a commitment, go for it. Give it everything you've got. The organization may not reward you (they may even ignore you) but you will be rewarding yourself by giving your all. Above all, do not let the numerous obstacles that hierarchies and bureaucracies create distract you or get you down.

Perseverance is key to maintaining any community and you are responsible for helping the community work out its problems.

Supporting the Members

This responsibility is in part an extension of one of the responsibilities to others. You help members by offering assistance with choices, which is in turn accomplished by listening, providing information and pointing out options. The difference has to do with the fact that if your community is large or spread out, you may not have personal contact with most of the members. In a very real sense, for example, I am the only known member of the Oregon Shakespeare Festival, because although the statistics I receive in the annual report show thousands of members, I have never met one of them and only see them when I attend plays in the summer. They are anonymous to me.

This anonymity is not important in and of itself, because we cannot possibly get to know every person on earth. The anonymity is only important if I have power over those faceless numbers. When this occurs, it is easy to dehumanize my relationship with them and avoid my responsibility to support them, for after all, they are simply numbers on a printout, figures on a balance sheet. This makes it easy to lay them off or send them to Auschwitz. They're just digits, not human beings who were living under the belief that they were a vital part of a community.

Muttering platitudes about how unfortunate it is to have to lay off people or how a company has to remain competitive in the marketplace does not excuse the action. This is self-justification of a very limited sort, usually supported by the silly old rule that one must leave one's emotions out of the decision-making process. The absence of face-to-face experience always presents the danger of irresponsible dehumanization, as does the deliberate exclusion of emotion from the decision-making process. Those in power have a responsibility to their fellow community members to support and sustain them by working with them to find better solutions than unilateral termination.

When I was an HR executive, I was the guy charged with implementing executive decisions on layoffs. The decision-making process behind layoff decisions was always truncated and incomplete. We focused on financial arguments and ignored the other effects, such as lower productivity resulting from low morale and steep training curves for the survivors who now had to learn how to fill in for those let go. We simply did not work hard enough to find alternatives to throwing people out on the street, largely because the group was trying to please only one segment of their community, the shareholders, who rarely if ever concern themselves with human elements that cannot be captured on a balance sheet.

Then I noticed that whenever a layoff was scheduled, most of the other executives would conveniently make themselves unavailable. Anything to avoid facing the real human impact of the decision! I heard of one manager at another company who drove to a worksite in a limo, dropped in for a few minutes to order the managers there to lay off a good percentage of their workforce that day and then sped off in comfort, leaving the managers behind to deliver the bad news. For a month or so after the layoffs, this executive refused to accept visitors or callers, allegedly out of fear that an unhappy employee would start shooting. What she failed to realize is that the distance itself engenders the powerlessness that employees sometimes feel and that sometimes leads them to take desperate actions.

Sometimes layoffs may be necessary. Sometimes executives are faced with the consequences of bad decisions made in the past. But to make a decision about someone else's life without considering all the options and without involving that person in the decision is fundamentally irresponsible. People in power have it tough, but they also have a responsibility to the people in the community to use their power responsibly in the best interests of all the members. It is more incumbent on the people in power therefore, to discipline themselves to live up to this responsibility by providing truthful information, listening to the needs of the members and by working with them to create options in any situation.

Meeting Obligations

Any community carries with it certain obligations. As a citizen of the United States, you have an obligation to pay your bills and obey the laws. When obligations go unmet, you are the one that experiences the unpleasant consequences, so why bother to attempt to avoid them? When communities consist of people who do not want to meet their obligations anymore, they fall apart, and while some communities deserve to fall apart (the French monarchy of the late 18th century for example), others do not. While there are certainly times when conscience leads a person to choose to disobey the law (as was common during the Vietnam War), it is usually better to keep one's nose clean as far as obligations go.

A better approach is to adopt the stance that the fewer obligations one has, the better off one will be. The most important decision-making variable always has to do with the purposes you are trying to achieve. If you can review every potential obligation through the question, "How is this going to help me realize my purposes?" you will be able to resist many unnecessary transactions. We enter into any of our financial obligations without much thought as we get caught in the fever of consumerism. With a little forethought, achieved by forcing ourselves to ask a few questions, we can learn to limit our obligations and give ourselves more room to maneuver.

Here are a few additional questions you can use to review potential obligations:

*   *   *

Reviewing Obligations

Why do I want to enter this obligation?
What is the time commitment behind this obligation?
How is this obligation going to restrict other choices I might want to make?

How is this going to help me achieve my purposes in the avenues I have chosen?

What alternatives exist to this particular obligation? Is there a less burdensome way for me to achieve the goal behind the obligation?

*   *   *

You owe it to yourself and your community to carefully weigh the pros and cons of your choices.

Quit When It's Time

The final consideration in developing a responsibility to a community has to do with the fact that things sometimes don't work out between you and your community. The problem with most people is that they never know when to quit. This is particularly true in the workplace.

There are several reasons why people hang on longer than they really should. Many people hate to give up, period. They do not want to feel that all their efforts have gone to waste. Others feel that they could have done more, saying to themselves, "If only I could have done this better or get these people to listen to me, things would have been different." In extreme cases, they blame themselves for the problem. Comfort certainly contributes to staying beyond the checkout time, as does the fear of change itself. Obligations play a part in keeping people where they are, for it is usually the over-obligated who are constantly willing to support the old cliché that "all companies are the same; it's not going to be better anywhere else." Some people lack confidence to make a move; others are completely unaware of the fact that they have options.

Once I traveled to a branch in one of the mid-western states to try to deal with an ongoing conflict between one of the staff and virtually everyone else in the office. The person in question had done nothing to deserve discipline or termination. She was just a constant pain-in-the-ass.

"Anal-retentive in the extreme," said the branch manager, engaging in some amateur psychologizing.

I then met with the anal-retentive pain-in-the-ass at the center of the controversy. After listening to her for awhile, I learned that she had taken this job years ago because there weren't any jobs for librarians at the time. She had graduated from college with a Master's of Library Science and was working as an administrative assistant in an office of unruly, fast-talking, money-hungry sales people. This was never going to work and it was time to face the facts.

So I looked her straight in the eyes and said, "You don't belong here. This isn't what you want to do and the environment is poison to you. You need to find a place more compatible with your abilities and your temperament. You can do better than this." No one had ever told her anything like that; apparently, friends and relatives had written her off as a lifetime clerk and she had lived up to their expectation of underachievement. The ongoing conflict was no one's fault per se; it was just a bad fit. I told her to let go of any feelings of failure she might have experienced in her frustration and simply realize that she belonged with other people who valued intellect, research skills and order. Right now she was working with people who valued success, competitiveness and chaos. After realizing it wasn't her fault and that she did in fact have options, she left the company about a month later, finding a job in a nearby research facility.

Here was an unnecessary conflict that had gone on for years primarily because she didn't know when to fold 'em. She had made an unwise choice to begin with, then became a martyr to the cause of bad choices. If she was going to live up to her responsibilities to self, other and community, she was going to have to review her choices more carefully.

Over the years I have dealt with dozens of people who didn't belong where they were. I have known frustrated artists and authors who were operating under the guilt that they had sold themselves out and took it out on the organization by being assholes to everyone around them. I have worked with high-level executives who had risen to the top by a series of lucky accidents and really wanted to go back to reviewing ledgers or pounding the pavement for sales. And of course there were numerous women who had been told for years that it was wrong for a woman to have a career and were holding down menial jobs far below their capabilities to help pay a mortgage. All of these people could have done better if they had been aware of their options, and both they and the organization would have been better off had they been given the confidence to consider those options.

To not know when it is time to leave is both irresponsible to yourself and to your community. You can avoid this situation if you carefully consider the symptoms that can indicate that it's time to make a graceful exit:

Value Conflicts: Experience tells me this is the primary cause of workplace unhappiness. Value conflicts cause people to experience sleepless nights and unproductive days. They are problematic because any conflict that remains on a values level is virtually impossible to resolve. If you are experiencing constant anger or disgust at management decisions and policies, if your boss is asking you to do things that you feel are unethical or in conflict with your personal beliefs, or if your conscience is needling you about working for a company that makes things or provides services that you feel are harmful, it's probably time to start looking.

Inexplicable Outbursts: If you find yourself flying off the handle at co-workers at the slightest provocation, or getting into frequent arguments about trivial issues, the anger you are feeling is probably misdirected. It is more likely that you are angry with yourself for having chosen your current job and are taking your frustrations out on the company instead of looking in a mirror. These kinds of outbursts are often a cry for help, as people tend to have a very hard time with two basic human needs: admitting a mistake and asking for assistance.

Boredom: While this should be self-explanatory, it isn't. Many people accept boredom as one of the unavoidable consequences of work. It has always been amazing that the human race tolerates the notion that work should be drudgery, but there is plenty of evidence to support it. I heard a typical conversation at the local coffee shop just this morning. "What have you been up to?" "Workin'" (Sigh.) "Yeah, me too." (Sigh.) In those sighs and in the lack of embellishment in describing the nature of a core human experience lies a tolerance for the idea that work is an inescapable penalty of life. It doesn't have to be that way. If you're bored, you owe it to yourself and your community to find something more engaging.

Cold Shoulders: You think things are going swimmingly but then you notice that people have begun avoiding you in the hallways. You are no longer invited to certain meetings or after-work drinking sessions. Friends tell you that rumors about you are rampant, particularly one that claims you have already left the company. What has happened is that some important mucky-muck has made an unfavorable comment about something you have done, and rather than deal with you directly, he or she has dropped the hint to a few lackeys that you are no longer in favor. Take the hint and leave. Consider it this way: why would you want to work for a company that allows its managers to avoid playing it straight with its people?

Summary

Responsibility to community demonstrates the interlinking of all three responsibilities. It is impossible to be responsible to self while being irresponsible to others and to the community because complete self-interest is never good for the individual. One cannot be responsible to others while ignoring responsibility to self, for becoming a sacrificial lamb to the expectations of other people serves no one. And one cannot be responsible solely to a community without being responsible to self and others, for a community thrives on the strength of its individuals and the relationships they forge together.

These three responsibilities represent a framework for a new perspective on organizational life. The predominant theory of organizational change says that organizations change when you change the systems, causing human behavior to adapt accordingly. Such a theory dehumanizes individuals, leaving them passive victims of forces beyond their control. Furthermore, it also allows people to escape responsibility with the too-obvious excuse that "it's the damned system." This sort of thinking makes people feel powerless and impotent, and a thriving culture needs people who are encouraged to think and act effectively. Given the contradictory nature of our current social debate on the subject of responsibility, where we constantly search for scapegoats while giving the truly guilty plenty of outs to enable them to escape consequences, we need to realize that the only way things are going to change is if we change them ourselves.

No one is going to do it for us. After all, organizations are human creations.

RESPONSIBILITY IN THE WORKPLACE

There are those of you who have gone through the exercises, reviewed the various options and applied some hard thinking to the matter only to reach the conclusion that your best bet is still the corporate environment. You may have concluded that corporations offer you the best chance for meeting your personal goals or you may have decided that due to other responsibilities you need some time to make a transition to something else. In either case, your choice has certain consequences for you.

First, those of you who have decided that corporate life is something you wish to escape need to accept that fact that you have chosen to be there. It may not have been your preferred choice and you may rather be doing something entirely different. This does not negate the original choice to work there and because you have made that choice, you owe it to yourself, the people you work with and the community of the corporation to live up to your responsibilities.

Second, whether you are there because you are in transition or because this is where you think you should be, you will inevitably encounter some of the unpleasant aspects of corporate life as described in the earlier chapters. Most people who come across these situations do one of two things: check out mentally, or gripe, gripe, gripe. Those options are certainly available to you, but there are important consequences you should consider before you begin posting Dilbert cartoons in your cubicle or taking potshots at the empty suits at the top of the hierarchy.

The most serious consequence to checking out or channeling your expressive energy into complaints is that you wind up hurting yourself. When you are on autopilot, you are not learning, growing or stretching yourself. When you are simply occupying space, you become stale, stagnant and out of touch. The cerebral muscle misses the exercise it needs and so becomes flaccid and lifeless. When you are not fully engaged, you miss opportunities, suffer from diminished responsiveness and often wind up more stuck than you were to begin with. Furthermore, by avoiding full engagement, you are in danger of planting a negative image of yourself in others, which could lead them to ignore your ideas entirely (after all, no one wants to sit around and listen to someone complain all day). If things change in your corporate leadership to reveal real possibilities for improvement, the new powers-that-be may not take you seriously. No matter what your circumstances are, no matter how bad the organization, you owe it to yourself to try to make a difference, if only to keep yourself awake to new possibilities and directions.

The negative side effects of avoiding engagement also extend to your relationships with others. The nasty energy you generate causes others around you to feel cynical as well. While talking with each other truthfully about the problems you face is to be encouraged, stopping the conversation before considering action only reinforces hopelessness. Complaining does not help anyone work through their choices and is therefore fundamentally irresponsible unless you can also answer the question, "What are we going to do about it?"

The community also suffers if you choose to check out. The corporation is essentially paying someone for not contributing, just as the government pays farmers not to grow crops. You are occupying space that someone else may want to fill, someone whose values, dreams and desires are more in line those of the company. By encouraging people to believe that the situation is hopeless, you increase the likelihood that the situation will always be hopeless. All communities thrive on the belief that what they are doing is achievable and important.

If you want to live responsibly for yourself, for others and for your workplace community, checking out is not a viable option. As long as you are there, you owe it to yourself, to others and to the community to give according to your talents and abilities. If it is time to leave, then leave, but don't just sit there and do nothing. Once you join any community, you are a part of it, so when you complain about the company, you are only complaining about yourself and broadcasting your inability to change things. When you hear someone say, "this place sucks," what you're really hearing is "I can't figure out how to get things done and so I'll blame someone else."

It is one thing to acknowledge a serious problem but it is another thing to throw our hands in the air and set to wailing. We deserve better than that.

Changing Organizations

Contrary to the belief in the organizational development profession, organizational change is not about changing systems. It isn't even really about changing people, for that implies coercion from a self-appointed higher consciousness who believes that people need changing. Organizational change is all about awakening the awareness in people that they can change things if they choose to do so. It involves recognizing that organizations are human creations created by human beings for human purposes. Once a significant number of people inside an organization see that, problems become solvable for the simple reason that the people in the organization realize that they are the ones who have created the mess they're in.

Having been the so-called driver behind several successful organizational change efforts, I can say with complete confidence that what changes organizations are not new systems, policies or technologies but the manifestation of human will. When people with a shared vision have confidence that they can create the organization they want to create, they do it. Organizational change work is about clarifying what people want the organization to be, removing real and perceived obstacles, clearing up old misunderstandings and above all, giving people confidence and permission that they can achieve what they want to achieve.

I have also been involved in a few less-than-successful change efforts. In every case, I could have done a much better job of gathering information, understanding the motivations of the people who had identified the need for change and making a compelling case for change to the rest of the organization. There were also times when I simply should have refused to participate in a proposed change effort, when I let my own personal desire to transform the world blind me to the impossibility of change within an existing power structure. However, just as I cannot take all the credit for the successes, I cannot take all the blame for the failures. When I look at the failures for another common variable, one stands out very clearly.

The leaders of the organization had serious hidden agendas and were therefore unwilling to either tell the truth or perceive the truth.

One of the leaders I worked with found it advantageous to be trendy. His peer group was definitely into cutting-edge stuff and during racquetball matches and rounds of golf would trade buzzwords over the latest developments in organizational change technology. Because it was important for him to be seen as a happening kind of guy, he wanted an organizational development effort that would raise him above his peers, thus compensating for humiliations on the court or slices into the sandtraps. His desire to stay current with business fashion conflicted with his hyperactive personality, which was controlling, aggressive and entirely alienating. He wanted hype, not change. As we started the process, which in this case involved extending decision-making power to line workers, his frequent and public explosions about what we were doing created a change effort that moved one step forward and two steps back.

Another leader I encountered wanted training for everyone else but not for him. He always talked about what "they needed to know," carefully excluding himself from the possibility that his own knowledge was less than adequate. Equipped with only a superficial understanding of the principles of effective leadership that we were trying to implement in the company, he wound up blocking nearly every change initiative generated by his subordinates. The life went out of that change effort very, very quickly.

The third leader was an interesting case. I completely misread his intentions, despite evidence that should have been as obvious as a smoking gun on a bedside table. Upon entering the organization, I met the leader and the top human resources person. They informed me that my main job would be to help the managers and employees prepare for major changes in the industry. They also told me that there were no significant problems with morale. When I began interviewing people in the organization, I found a radically different interpretation of reality. These were the unhappiest people I had ever met. They were completely frustrated with management and with each other, stressed from working long hours, bitter about several company decisions and hopeless about any possibility of improvement. When I confronted the HR executive about this perceptual gap, he responded by saying, "Well, if we'd told you the truth, you wouldn't have come." In my findings, I laid the situation out as I read it, pulling no punches and positioning nothing. The leader refused to talk to me afterwards. I had a hard time getting anyone to return my phone calls and for obvious reasons, I did not get the contract.

Perhaps I could have positioned the situation in a way that might have made the data more palatable and thereby sewn up the deal. However, if I would have done that, things would have been worse for all concerned. The change effort would have been marked by interruptions and contradictions that would have only reconfirmed the general feeling that things were hopeless. I would have been compromising my integrity by working with an organization that did not want to deal with facts. The leader's blindspots would have blocked any attempt at real change and exposing them through a change effort might have been too painful and embarrassing for him. Lacking self-confidence and the ability to self-reflect, he wanted to believe that he was great and that everyone in the organization thought things were great without doing the work it really takes to become great.

The essential message of these stories is this: *it is extremely difficult to change an organization if the people in power do not want to change the organization.* This is as true for societies as it is for organizations, as the example of Dr. Martin Luther King demonstrates. The changes wrought by Dr. King took years of patience, perseverance and fight. They required a willingness to risk physical and psychological harm. It took a great deal of skill to communicate and sustain a vision based on shared values that could link those on opposite sides of the civil rights question. Finally, Dr. King was a great man but even he knew he could not achieve his dream alone. He needed to enlist the support of others to realize the common goal.

The risks you face in trying to change a corporation will not be as intimidating as those Dr. King faced. However, you do face the same dynamic in terms of the resistance you will face from those on top. The authority granted to leaders in hierarchies give them enormous negative power and they can effectively block any changes that do not suit their tastes. The inherent conservatism of leaders in a hierarchy is partly because they want to protect the community from harm and partly because they want to protect their own personal agendas. If you are in an organization where the leaders are insecure, defensive, and arrogant, exhibiting such qualities through their distance, explosions or insistence on superficial communication, the best you can hope for is incremental, small-scale change, usually within the boundaries of your department. If you are in an organization where your leaders think they know everything, have neither the ability nor inclination to engage in self-reflection or whose actions reveal that they do not care about people, it will be difficult to realize change, no matter what you do.

However, let us not be too hasty on this subject. People often give up too quickly on their leaders, using one or two examples of the arbitrary use of power to justify inaction. Every leader is capable of making poor decisions and sometimes the decisions leaders face are extremely problematic. We often make unfair judgments about certain decisions because we do not know all the facts. The leader, limited in what he or she can share due to legal restrictions or common decency, may not be able to provide all the information. The point is: do not give up on a leader too quickly, for not only may things be different than they seem, but some leaders can and do change over time.

Even if the pattern shows that your top people are permanently out to lunch and put more energy into preserving their perks than making things better, you still may not have to leave, either physically or mentally. There remain actions you can take to live up to all of your responsibilities and do some good for your community in the bargain.

What to Do When Your Leaders Seem Hopeless

Before you decide it's time to turn the lights out, you owe it to yourself, your co-workers and your community to try something to raise the awareness of your leadership that things need to change. Here are a few of the things I have seen work at various companies:

Treat the Leader Like a Human Being: The distance between our leaders and us does not come entirely from the top. We inject distance into the relationship ourselves by exalting leaders. Some people approach leaders as if they were approaching a throne on a scarlet carpet, in humble silence and with great obsequiousness. Others use the distance to give themselves psychological permission to trash the leader, since it is always easier to attack someone who is either distant or invisible.

While some of them go to great lengths to deny it, leaders are no different than other human beings. They like to be heard and they like it when people show interest in what they have to say. Contrary to popular opinion, leaders do not always appreciate toadies who are quick to agree them, largely because it is so obvious that it becomes embarrassing.

Try to forge a non-judgmental relationship with your leader. When you ask questions, don't pose them as if you were a reporter at a presidential press conference, contaminating the request for information with implications of incompetence and corruption. Listen carefully and ask good clarifying questions, avoiding the tendency to use questions as an opportunity to show a leader how wonderful you are. If a leader feels listened to, he or she will tend to share more and be more open to listening to your ideas.

One final caution regarding communicating with leaders. Never show up a leader in front of a group. A leader is in the most vulnerable position in the group because the leader is the most visible and identifiable member. That is a risky proposition for anyone and leaders often become lightning rods for discontent. When that discontent turns into a mob mentality in a group setting, chances are that you will shut down the leader for good.

Approach the Problem from a "We Standpoint": No one, leaders included, reacts positively to the presentation of a problem when it is accompanied by finger-pointing. By blaming others or by stating the problem so neutrally that blame-seeking people can jump to the conclusion that someone is at fault, you will get nowhere. Furthermore, leaders have a learned aversion to problems because they often have more of them than they know what to do with. Preface any presentation of a situation with "we," as in "we have a problem." This communicates shared responsibility, ensures the leader that he or she is not alone and makes them feel good that someone (yourself) has done some thinking about what to do. Such an approach makes bad news acceptable by making the problem seem solvable. "We" can always solve problems more effectively than "you."

Make it Their Idea: Sometimes you will have to deal with bulging egos in your dealings with leaders. If this is the case, look for an opportunity to make them look good in front of the people whose opinions they value. When problems arise, introduce your idea by referring back to some of their comments or opinions on the topic, then tie that to your suggestion to make it look like the idea was a natural consequence of their penetrating thought. You may have to stretch a bit to make the connection, but if you work hard enough, you should be able to find one.

Learn Their Parameters I know a very successful mid-level manager who adopted a good strategy for dealing with his somewhat autocratic leader by defining boundaries. The first thing he did was to stop taking the leader's controlling tendencies personally, a critical first step. The second step he took was to stop assuming that his leader was controlling about every issue. Often we use the phenomenon of extension when forming our perceptions of leaders, using one bad quality or one bad situation to form a general impression of a leader that excuses us from taking action. Instead of extending the autocrat label to everything associated with his leader, he sat down with him and learned the leader's parameters by asking some very focused questions:

What are your priorities?

What do I need to do to satisfy you?

What do you need to do to satisfy your boss?

What will you not tolerate from a direct report?

What kinds of things hit your hot buttons?

What changes are you unwilling to entertain?

By identifying what parts of the field were unplayable, he managed to identify those areas where he was free to make changes, and by gaining the leader's support in those areas, was able to forge a workable relationship.

Put Your Leader in the Job Market: If all else fails, if you are constitutionally unable to consider the leader as anything more than your enemy, if you are certain you have given the leader a fair chance and if you are convinced that the leader will never change and is the primary obstacle to improvement, you may want consider this option. I know a group (a purchasing department, it was) who (with the help of the leader's administrative assistant, who was also sick of the leader in question) sent copies of his resume to several headhunters. About three months later, the leader had landed a job in another organization and everyone was happy.

This brings up some interesting ethical questions. After all, is it kosher to "borrow" someone's resume to get rid of them? On the other hand, if a leader is guilty of the arbitrary and excessive use of power, shopping his or her resume is a far more gentle way to resolve the situation than staging a coup. To keep your responsibilities clear, I would suggest you only use this method if you have confronted the leader directly about the need for change the exchange brought forth no hope. In this situation, your responsibility to the community becomes paramount, for you have lived up to your responsibility to the other (the leader) and now have the right to consider other options. You may have to live with the guilt related to pawning a bad leader off on another company, but then again, that leader may improve with a change of scenery.

Go Over Their Heads: Of all the options I have listed, this is my least favorite, but I will give you the rationale for it anyway. Since hierarchies operate under the chain-of-command with the misguided notion that those above are somehow responsible for those below, you do have the option of approaching the leader's boss about problems you are having with the leader (unless, of course, the leader in question is the CEO). This is an essential step when you suspect legal or ethical violations, for you have a responsibility to your community to stop an unethical leader from destroying it.

But what if your leader is acting perfectly within the law and any known moral code but is simply using the position to block progress? What if your leader is like a supervisor I once knew, a person who prided himself on his tough-guy approach by saying, "I'm fair. Damned fair. I treat everyone on my staff equally badly." In this situation, you have the option of going over his or her head but it usually doesn't work. Managers who are controlling and dictatorial value absolute authority and unquestioned loyalty. When you go over the head of such a person, he or she will likely view you as a traitor, and while the attempt may yield some short-term relief for your work group, the leader will probably never forget or forgive what you have done. I cannot recall ever seeing a manager initiate any self-reflection or real long-term improvement as the result of an employee going to his boss about him. Usually, they lay low for a few months and then come back as obnoxious as ever.

If you are considering this option, emboldened perhaps by a company policy that says that is okay to do that, consider the personality of your leader's boss before you go marching into his or her office with your list of demands. I would suggest avoiding this option if that leader is either too weak to do anything about the problem, insufficiently skilled to coach your boss through an improvement plan or cut from the same dictatorial cloth as his or her subordinate.

Setting Your Own Example

One extremely powerful catalyst for changing organizations is the presence of people within the organization who maintain their integrity through even the most difficult circumstances. We look at these people while bullets are flying all around us and tell ourselves, "Well, it can't be that bad, so-and-so's still here."

The long and short of it is that you cannot change an organization if you are participating in the status games, controlling others through power and procedure, avoiding truth with the expertise of a political press secretary or otherwise failing to live up to any of your responsibilities. Only by remaining true to yourself can you hope to have any impact on others or on your community.

Probably the most important contribution you can make to your community is to keep your skills sharp. By staying in touch with the latest developments in your profession, you reduce the risk of becoming stale while refreshing the organization with new ideas and perspectives. Self-development is an aspect of self-responsibility with enormous positive impact on your community. It also serves as an example of other community members to follow, thereby strengthening the entire group.

In the area of your responsibility to others, open, honest and relevant communication is the foundation of any serious attempt to change an organization. By avoiding the impulse to join in the ever-present chorus of blame, you set yourself apart as someone who is serious about making a difference. You also present yourself to others as someone they can approach without feeling judged. When people get together in a non-judgmental environment, it is astonishing how many new ideas and possibilities they can generate for the betterment of all.

These actions roll up into the overriding responsibility you have to your community. By avoiding the blame game and developing yourself, you are supporting your fellow community members in their efforts to make a difference. By meeting your commitments and refusing to let them slide simply because everyone else does, you maintain the hope that things can change within your organization. By demonstrating a commitment to fight the necessary battles instead of surrendering to the impotence of mere complaining, you sustain the consciousness of community for others as well as yourself.

The presence of integrity, as manifested through actions that demonstrate a commitment to all three areas of responsibility, will usually outlast all the crazy, turbulent and absurd periods that every organization endures. Staying with an organization may mean making certain compromises in your personal life, but it never means you have to compromise your integrity.

General Wisdom

In your daily existence inside an organization, you will no doubt come across unexpected problems and surprising opportunities. You will face a number of situations where you may not be sure what to do. These situations are identifiable by the presence of what I call the "organizational hiccup," a moment where time seems to freeze and paralysis replaces action. Your responsibilities seem to be in conflict with each other.

What usually causes the hiccup is uncertainty and a lack of confidence in dealing with uncertainty. What you have to realize is that it is not the uncertainty itself that is the problem but the unreasonable expectation we have that things be certain and predictable. They are not now and it is highly doubtful that they have ever been. What used to represent certainty for us were merely unquestioned assumptions and unchallenged beliefs. Many beliefs and assumptions are being questioned now due to cultural and technological change, which in turn reveal the old certainties as comfortable and convenient illusions rather than rock-solid truths.

Since most of life is an experiment anyway, feel free to forge right ahead into the uncertainty and suggest a way of dealing with the problem of the moment. When faced with the unexpected, speculate, probe, ask questions, get others to help you scope out the situation. Believe it or not, you are not the only one experiencing the uncertainty, so don't be fooled by other people covering up their fear of exposed ignorance by pretending to know what's going on. Approach problems with wonder and courage, not fear and avoidance.

The next tip on general workplace responsibility is simple but difficult: *ask for help when you need it.* I once supervised a group of highly responsible and conscientious people with superior teamwork—except when it came to individuals asking other individuals for help when they were in a bind. It is hard for us to admit that we need help. All the cultural conditioning around being "tough" and "doing it my way" has distorted our notion of self-reliance. Forget that stuff. Everyone needs help from time to time and it is your responsibility to forgive yourself for your weaknesses and your co-workers' responsibility to lend that assistance.

Another precept often ignored in the workplace is to *go to the person with whom you have a problem.* Often when someone pisses us off we tell others, most likely looking for someone to validate our perceptions of the inherent evil in the other person. We avoid telling the person in question, rationalizing it in many ways from "it's not nice to hurt another person's feelings" to "they'll never listen anyway." Avoiding direct communication is always ineffective, leading you to make unreal assumptions about that person that move you further and further from reality. If someone has upset you, be it your leader or a co-worker, confront them directly and give them a chance to explain. You will probably discover that your perceptions were not entirely accurate and that there was a rational explanation for why a person did what they did. Delivering a whole message and then listening carefully to the response can not only solve the immediate problem but enhances the possibility of better cooperation in the future.

Summary

The relationship of a human being to his or her work is a complex one. It can be a source of immense satisfaction or burdensome toil. Work can be exciting and meaningful or dull and empty. While we use work to produce the income that allows us to increase our choices in a capitalistic economy, we also use work as a fundamental means of self-expression. While you are more than what you do, it is also true that through your work you give to the world a bit of who you are.

It is common in our culture to complain about the work we do. I was on the metro the other day when I heard two people strike up a conversation about their work.

She: How's the job?
He: Sucks. I hate my boss.
She: Well, that's normal. Everybody hates their boss. I mean, mine's okay but well, you know.
He: Yeah. I don't know. I'm thinking of looking.
She: What would you be looking for?
He: I don't know. I don't know if I like what I'm doing but I don't know what I really want to do.
She: Yeah, I know how that is.

He: Work sucks.
She: Yeah.

Although this would strike most people as a fairly commonplace interchange of no consequence, it was anything but trivial. These people were talking about their gut-level dissatisfaction with one of our most fundamental activities. They felt frustrated with the workplace but could not figure out what to do about that frustration. Underlying the words was a surrender to the notion of "that's the way things are, learn to live with it." They entered into the world of work through a default choice and suffered the consequences. Their experience is one shared by millions of working people who experience the same feelings every working day.

Instead of saying, "there's nothing we can do about it," this book has tried to point out the existence of viable alternatives. We can avoid organizations altogether or we can work to change them. Instead of saying "too bad, you made your bed and now you have to lie in it," this book has tried to point out the importance of compassion in helping each other transform our frustrations into more positive actions. While workplaces will never be perfect, human creations that they are, we can make them much more supportive of the people who sustain them by learning to make conscious choices about what we are doing and why we are doing it. It simply isn't good enough to continue to condemn ourselves to lifetimes spent in meaningless environments while we wish for miracles and lotteries to free us from the chains of work.

We can do a whole lot better.

About the Author

Bob Mendonsa is a consultant, trainer and coach in the fields of human potential and organizational change. When he is not working, Bob is a musician, poet, father and something of a romantic. Bob lives and works in San Francisco.

For more information about the business side of Bob, visit http://www.trainingplus.com

Appendix

Appendix: Working Arenas

There are two major considerations in choosing your primary means of generating income. The usual consideration is the nature of the work itself and the specific qualities of certain jobs. The field of career development focuses on this choice and has made significant strides over the last ten years in helping people define desired occupations. However, there is a second consideration we often miss. This is the arena in which you will do your work. The arena is the broader working environment in which you find particular jobs. This section deals with the most common arenas in existence today.

Both the selected occupation and the chosen arena have an enormous impact on job satisfaction. We know that different occupations in the same arena involve different experiences of the working day. For example, although accountants and salespersons may share the same corporate space, the nature of their work is quite different, which in turn means that their daily reality is also different. What we often fail to appreciate is that the experience of work differs significantly with the arena in which we perform the work. An accountant in an arts organization, for example, is going to have a different working experience than our corporate number-cruncher because the rules of the game, the structure and the general feel of an arts organization is very different from the corporate environment.

To make a decent choice regarding your employment, you need to gather enough information about both the arena and the nature of the job. This segment gives some pluses and minuses of various arenas to give you a head start in determining which is the healthiest place for you to be.

Although there is hardly enough space in this book to discuss the unique realities of particular occupations, there are some excellent resources available in the career counseling section of your bookstore. In addition to researching that field, balance your study with real world contact. Go out and interview at least three people who are working in your field of interest. Don't limit yourself to questions about the superficial aspects of the job such as money and status. Dig deeper into the day-to-day working reality so you can see if the job is a fit for your temperament. Some sample questions you can use include the following:

Describe a typical day, week or month on the job.

What percentage of time do you spend dealing with people and what percentage of time do you spend working alone?

What is satisfying about the work itself?

What is frustrating about the work itself?

What personal qualities are important in being successful at this kind of work? (patience? perseverance? quick-thinking? ability to shrug off insults? manual dexterity?)

Your goal in these interviews is to get a realistic picture of the daily reality of a given occupation. This is important because a common complaint of many professional people is "I thought it would be different." Idealists who become attorneys experience disillusionment when exposed to crassness of legal wheeling and dealing. People who want to help others may find they have little tolerance for getting screamed at all day by angry customers and clients. Salespeople who envisioned a life of dynamic freedom find themselves frustrated by mountains of paperwork. While you can never obtain perfect information to enable you to make a perfect choice, you will move closer to achieving your goals if you gather enough data as to the true nature of the work.

Once you have done that and are relatively certain you want to try your hand at that kind of work, you then need to consider the arena where you will be doing your work.

Arenas

What follows is a review of the major employment arenas currently available to the average person. We discuss the pluses and minuses associated with each arena so that in reviewing your avenues you can make intelligent choices as to what kind of environment will work best for you. The major arenas discussed are as follows:

The Arts
Corporations
Education
Government
Independent Practice
The Military
Non-profit Organizations
Small Business
Start-ups
Volunteer Work

I have excluded one major arena, religion, because the motivation to pursue work in that particular arena can only be evaluated from within.

You will no doubt have your own interpretation of the situations common to these arenas. It is also possible that you may not consider the minuses as real drawbacks but simply obstacles to overcome as you move towards your goal. If that is the case, check yourself to make sure you are not simply being stubborn because of an old expectation like "I've always wanted to be a teacher," but that you truly possess a driving sense of purpose.

For if you have that sense of purpose, you might be able to change "reality" and make a difference.

The Arts

This section covers the lives of those we classify as artists. Arts administrators should check out the section on non-profit organizations. The classification of artist is something that is quite arbitrary, for I have experienced what I would call "artistic insights" while teaching and communicating just as often as I have experienced them with a paintbrush or my guitar. There is the opportunity for artistry in many occupations; in this section, however, we will focus more on the traditional definitions of artist.

What sustains the artist is the passion for the art, be it plastic, performing or literary art. You need that passion to sustain you because most artists do not make money during their lifetimes and nearly always have to take part-time or full-time employment to survive. This is true for actors, for painters, for dancers, for musicians. The likelihood of relative poverty is present even in those areas where social trends support popular consumption of the art, as with filmmaking or rock 'n' roll. Making it in those industries often depends more on chance, a quirky smile or the willingness to be outrageous than real talent.

Having been an average poet, songwriter and musician—and a dreadful painter—I can say without a doubt that the most satisfying experiences in life lie in the act of creation. Seeking recognition beyond the fulfillment of the creative vision is usually a frustrating experience for most artists, because the overriding responsibility of being true to oneself is most acutely felt by those with artistic yearnings. A lifetime in the arts can only be sustained by the joy of the creative act; if recognition comes, great; if it doesn't, you have been compensated by one of the most wondrous of all human experiences.

Pluses

+ There is tremendous freedom in being an artist. People expect you to be a bit off-center, so you can bend social limitations more easily than those identified with traditional occupation.

+ There is nothing like the joy of creation, the flash of insight and the emergence of the unique within the structural limitations of the art form.

+ Artists do not lead ordered lives. They frequently work on temporary assignments or as part-time employees with flexible schedules. The vast part of the artist's routine comes from self-discipline.

+ Great art has always had the power to move people, to change perceptions, to expand awareness.

Minuses

- Creative blockages are common to artists, in part because they are frequently torn between what they want to do and what their patrons and public want them to do, and in part because of self-doubt. These blank periods can be extremely frustrating.

- Many artists are relatively poor people. The handful of actors who land million dollar contracts, the smattering of artists who are featured in major shows and the few musicians who appear regularly on MTV are a decided minority. Dancers and poets have virtually no opportunity to make money at their craft, while actors and writers receive very little return for their investments in auditions and queries.

- Artistic communities can be very status-oriented within the community, particularly when dominated by people who feel the need to be at the forefront of a movement.

- Funding problems for the arts have increased, which means fewer opportunities for musicians, dancers, actors and other artists who align themselves with non-profit organizations.

Corporations

We covered life in the corporate world in the first half of the book. We list the pluses and minuses here for easy reference.

Pluses

+   Corporations still represent the best balance of risk and reward in a purely economic sense. The risk is nowhere near what it is in self-employment and the rewards are both predictable and based on a relatively constant labor market. Corporations that offer stock options increase the opportunity for one to accumulate wealth.

+   You can meet some great people working in a corporation.

+   The business world offers some excitement if you are into competition, strategy and the notion of winning.

+   Hierarchies by nature offer opportunities for advancement, although these may be shrinking as corporations flatten.

+   Many modern corporations offer state-of-the-art training and equipment, which aids in personal development and job satisfaction.

+   Some companies offer job sharing, flexible scheduling and telecommuting. These arrangements can be significant considerations for parents or for single people who want maximum flexibility to explore other avenues.

Minuses

-    Never forget for one second that a corporation exists to make a profit (or at least to appear to shareholders that they are likely to make a profit). Profit towers above all other considerations in a corporation, flowery vision statements notwithstanding. If you become surplus, consideration for your loyalty and contribution will end with the severance package.

-    Corporations are infected with excessive preoccupation regarding status, expend great quantities of energy trying to control the behavior of their employees, live with very confused notions of leadership and create an environment where people avoid the truth. These problems affect everyone in the organization, for everyone in the organization gets caught up in the games sooner or later.

- Corporations often forget that they exist for human beings. The profit motive is itself a human motive. Neglect of the human factor creates the absurd environment that often pervades many organizations and leads employees to feel dehumanized.

Education

This section encompasses all the organizations and institutions traditionally associated with education. We are primarily looking at the schools, from elementary to secondary to colleges and universities; public or private; conventional or alternative.

The greatest downside to pursuing a career in education is that is the field most susceptible to blame and finger-pointing in our entire society, which means it is the arena where the issue of responsibility is most convoluted. Everyone agrees that American students could be getting a better education but no one agrees on how we can reach that goal. Parents blame teachers and administrators. Teachers blame parents for not taking a more active role in the education of their children and blame administrators for tying their hands. Administrators blame teachers' unions and government mandates regarding testing and textbooks. Politicians get into the fray and blame everyone in sight. The victims of all this are, of course, the children, and their boredom and frustration only becomes more ammunition for whichever faction wants to use it to their advantage.

My children attend public schools and I have to say the results are decidedly mixed. They have had a few excellent teachers, but even those teachers have seen their ability to teach compromised by the problem of too many students in the classroom. The textbooks have been uniformly dull and unexciting in every subject. Both of my sons have learned more from their parents, from exposure to various media (yes, even video games) and from attending various cultural events than they have in school. The educational game has not changed much from Charles Handy's description of his early education:

> The man stood in front of the class. "Now learn this," he said, writing an equation on the board. We wrote it in our books. Three months later we wrote it out again in an examination paper. If the second writing was the same as the first, we had learnt it. I exaggerate but only a little. That was my early concept of learning. Later on, I came to realize that I had learned nothing at school which I now remember except this—that all the problems had already been solved, by someone, and that the answer was around, in the back of the book or in the teacher's head. Learning seemed to mean transferring answers from them to me.

If I conducted my training classes using the same process, I'd never make a dime. Our system produces children groomed to pass obsolete tests allegedly measuring their scholastic aptitude so they can secure a spot on the career assembly line.

This is not going to change any time soon. Public education is unavoidably fettered to the corrupt political environment of the current era. Most less-than-upper-middle-class parents cannot afford to send their kids to private schools. There is also a legitimate question as to whether private schools are automatically better. They certainly give the parents status credits to use with their peers and some may do a better job of preparing kids for the SAT, but whether that translates into a better education is open to debate.

With this rather lengthy caution in mind, let us review the pluses and minuses of working in an apparently hopeless situation.

Pluses

+ Education presents an opportunity to make a real difference in people's lives, both in the present and in the future.
+ If the teacher combines a passion for helping others with an equally intense focus on self-development, education can be a growthful and beneficial experience.
+ Teaching well is a fundamentally creative experience.
+ Once a teacher achieves tenure, job security is virtually assured.
+ For those working in schools on traditional schedules, there is an annual opportunity for a long vacation.

Minuses

- Public schools are often underfunded, with poor facilities and equipment.
- Teachers are role models for children. Current mores require teachers to be as sanitized as Disney characters, free from vice or deviation of any kind. In many districts, controversy arises when it is discovered that a teacher is gay or lesbian, out of the absurd fear that the teacher is somehow going to contaminate the children. Education is not a nurturing field for those with lifestyles that do not fit into the narrow band of normality.
- The education process is highly politicized, full of blame and conflict and held hostage to whichever special interest group showed up at the board meeting first.
- Depending on the administration, teachers pretty much have to stick to the plan, use the inadequate textbooks furnished by the district and live within whatever restrictions imposed by the current climate.
- While long vacations are still possibilities (though dying off as year-round schooling becomes more common), teachers work around the clock during the school year, grading papers, preparing

lesson plans, dealing with unruly parents and children, and trying to please the administration.

- University environments are in particular quite status-conscious, with clear delineation as to professorial position. Some professors are so self-important that they delegate all instruction to teacher's aides.

Government

Working for the government has not been a viable option for some time, probably not since Kennedy energized a good portion of that era's younger generation to pursue careers in public service. Government organizations at every level are cutting back, with hiring at present limited to prisons, customs and critical positions opened through turnover. Government employees have a terrible reputation, with pejorative labels ranging from "bureaucrats" to "disgruntled postal workers." These labels are inherently unfair, as are all stereotypes. It is more accurate to say that government suffers from a vacuum of credible leadership due to the current political climate and it is fundamentally demotivating to work for leaders whose competence, commitment and integrity are often in question.

Although my graduate degree is in Public Administration, I have never worked in government. This is due to several influences. I went through the program with dozens of people who were working in various government entities, from police to public transportation to federal agencies, and to this day I have never seen a more bitter or disillusioned group of people in my life. In my various jobs in human resources, I have had contact with a number of government agencies, and while there are some extremely conscientious and motivated people interested in solving problems, the majority has been rulebound, paperbound and generally uncommunicative. I also have a dear friend in the Midwest who has been working for the federal government for over a decade. She describes an environment where people are astonishingly incompetent but cannot get fired, where grade-level status is a major issue and where the work performed is often unconnected to any visible purpose or outcome. The application process for government jobs is incredibly tedious when compared to that of the simple just-sub-mit-a-resume process of the corporate world, turning off many potentially valuable public servants. This does not signal that the people who work for government are bad, bureaucratic boobs, but that the leadership in most governmental entities suffers from too much political influence and too little creativity and courage.

Pluses

+ Certain government opportunities can be intensely meaningful: police, fire, the Peace Corps, environmentally related jobs, social work, scientific research, international relations, space exploration and the like. The emphasis again is on the phrase "can be," for here we are talking about the nature of the jobs themselves, inde-pendent of organizational manipulation.

+ Many government jobs pay relatively well, offer good benefits (particularly retirement) and are relatively stable (though this is changing rapidly).

+ Government is probably ahead of the rest of society in providing opportunities for women and minorities.

Minuses

- People who work for the government have to deal with the fact that the clients they serve are part of a society that views govern-ment employees in an unfavorable light.

- Even those government occupations supported by society are under pressure from the general cost-cutting mentality of today's voters. Voters who say they like the police and fire departments or their public libraries will turn around and cut city budgets to the bone.

- This is the most stifling working environment of all, particu-larly in large agencies. Endless procedures. Duplication of effort. High sensitivity to status, particularly in the GS-oriented federal institutions.

- Government suffers from a complete and continual vacuum of leadership. Most government leaders since the Watergate era have been elected in part by attacking the very employees they wish to lead. How would you like to work for someone whose stated goals are to cut your budget, cut your perks and even cut your job?

Independent Practice

This is what I do for a living at present, so I am intimately familiar with the benefits and risks. There are a lot of people doing consulting these days, but what many of them are really doing is giving themselves a socially acceptable label for an unexpectedly lengthy period of unemployment. This section is for people who want to set up an independent practice in a field where they have some expertise, which can be anything from counseling to management consulting to contract programming to any one-person business. What distinguishes this section from the section on small business is the absence of employees, who provide a whole separate set of pluses and minuses all by themselves.

The classification "entrepreneur" is a bridge between "independent practitioner" and "small business," so check that section if you consider yourself a potential entrepreneur.

Pluses

+ Although you have to maintain some reasonable form of office hours so people can get in touch with you, independent practice gives you a great deal more flexibility in setting your hours than working in an organization. You can structure your work around your personal body clock instead of the eight-to-five madness. For example, I take naps in the afternoon and work late into the night. However, I take my naps in my office so if a customer calls I am there to answer.

+   No one else's policies, procedures or rules govern your daily existence if you work in your own space. If you work at home, you don't even have to get dressed to go to work.

+   You do have to depend upon various vendors for supplies, equipment and the like, but generally it's easier to get things done when you're really a customer instead of just some jerk in another department.

+   You are answerable for everything in your work and no one can screw it up for you.

Minuses

-     You are answerable for everything in your work and no one can screw it up for you.

-     Marketing can be very problematic for many independent practitioners. Some do not feel comfortable in a sales role. Others feel uncomfortable talking about themselves.

-     Managing your own business can take a lot of time and energy. You will work harder on your own for the simple reason that no one else is there to pull your rear end out of the mud when you slip. If you're sick, tough. If a personal emergency comes up, tough. You have to respond effectively to customers, regardless of the inconvenience.

-     Cash flow is often uneven, taxes are significantly higher and you have to pay for all of your benefits. These factors put many first-time practitioners used to regular paychecks and corporate benefits into severe shock.

-     You feel you can never turn down a job because you never know if an assignment will be canceled. This can lead to overwork and burnout.

The Military

I have never served in the military. During the Vietnam era, I was classified as a conscientious objector by the Selective Service due to my unyielding opposition to killing other human beings in anything short of self-defense. I also believe there are other more peaceful ways of serving one's country that do not require a person to risk his or her life or the life of others.

But my values regarding war do not blind me to the fact that many very decent people have served and do serve in the armed forces, and that many of those people believe it is honorable to risk it all for one's country. I can respect that. Furthermore, I can certainly respect that the military teaches the self-discipline one needs to be successful at anything. This has a tremendous value in a culture where many kids never learn self-discipline from their over-indulgent workaholic parents.

Pluses

+   The military offers training in a variety of useful skills such as electronics and communications.

+   The military will virtually pay for a college education, making it a viable option for people who don't know what to do with themselves once they leave high school.

+   Veterans have many workplace protections, including reinstatement rights and (in government) favored hiring status.

+   The military offers one the chance to work in close quarters with people from diverse backgrounds. For many people, the military offers a first real experience of shared responsibility and teamwork with people who are "different."

+   The development of discipline, particularly self-discipline, is one of the virtues of military service.

+   Many veterans have found the experience to be a meaningful part of their lives.

Minuses

- There is always the risk of combat and the risks associated with combat. The United States often sends troops on peacekeeping missions in dangerous areas.
- The old macho tough guy mentality still exists in many quarters; hazing rituals have been exposed as an ongoing problem.
- The physical training is quite difficult (although masochists may find this appealing).
- The military invades one's personal life like no other institution in America. Ask gays, lesbians or heterosexuals who dare to commit that most human act of falling in love with each other.
- You will never get rich working in the military, so if that's your life ambition, seek your reward elsewhere.
- The military is a bureaucracy, and like all bureaucracies, can thoroughly dehumanize people. Numeric projections of casualties and the denial of knowledge regarding hazards faced by soldiers in battle are examples of the kind of thinking that is hardly comforting There are negative stereotypes regarding veterans that exist in many workplaces, over and above the prejudice that affected so many veterans returning from Vietnam. Rigid people who happen to have served in the military feed the stereotype that everyone who was in the military is automatically controlling. Nothing could be further from the truth; some of the kindest and most flexible people I have worked with have been veterans. Those who demand order in daily life will cherish the order found in the military, which has a natural attraction for such people. This does not mean that everyone who joins the military has a fetish for order. However, the perception exists and represents one of those special challenges we discussed earlier.

Non-profit Organizations

Non-profit organizations are not free of the problems faced in most corporations. Since many of them are always on the verge of going broke, there is a significant preoccupation with money, often at the expense of the underlying purpose of the organization. Being the poor cousin in the organizational family, non-profits generally do not pay as well as corporations or even government entities. Because no one is making money, some non-profits resort to status as a means of psychological compensation (manifested in artistic or mission-related snobbery). Still, a purposeful non-profit organization that is passionate about its mission without becoming religiously dogmatic can be a viable option for people whose priorities are more suited to making a difference in the world than making money.

Pluses

+   Many of these organizations offer a real purpose that is not simply about making money.

+   The purpose itself can be highly motivating, giving people a reason to come to work every day.

+   Small non-profits give people the opportunity to practice numerous skills, largely because there are never enough people in the non-profit to do what needs to be done.

+   Non-profits are more likely to build camaraderie within the organization than profit-making entities, again largely because of the energy associated with purpose.

+   Non-profits, particularly those associated with the arts, tend to encourage creativity more naturally than corporations. Those associated with social causes tend to encourage the "can do" spirit.

+   Smaller non-profits tend to rely less on formalized roles and procedures than large non-profits (and, of course, government and corporations).

Minuses

- You probably won't make a whole lot of money, particularly in the smaller organizations; benefits can be weak or non-existent.
- Non-profits that get paranoid about financial survival have the tendency to drift away from their purpose, which often hurts the organization's attempts to raise money, making the situation even worse.
- Board-staff relations are often problematic. Board members mean well, but they often don't know what to do with themselves. This can mean new and unrealistic initiatives for an overworked staff, or a complete lack of direction and support.
- You will probably work harder in a non-profit because staffing is frequently of the bare-bones variety.
- Arts groups tend to encourage snobbery. Social cause groups tend to encourage excessive dogma. All non-profit groups tend to encourage those annoying mailings and solicitations that prey on guilt surrounding failed community responsibilities.
- Leaders are often untrained in how to deal with people. This can be an advantage, since they avoid most of the behavioral conditioning corporate managers receive that renders them incapable of dealing with real people. Sometimes, however, non-profit leaders rely solely on their passion for the organization's mission, and while that can lend enthusiasm to the pursuit of the goal, it can also lead to tyranny when the leader envisions him or herself as the only one who can keep the torch burning.

Small Business

For purposes of this discussion, we will define a small business as a profit-oriented organization where everyone knows everybody else but which is not funded by large investors or venture capitalists.

Pluses

+   Small businesses avoid the impersonal nature of larger corporations simply because they are small and usually exist in a single physical location.

+   There are usually fewer rules, regulations and protocol in a small business than in a large corporation.

+   There is more visibility as to the impact of one's efforts than exists in larger organizations.

+   The opportunity to develop regular relationships with customers is much greater in a small business than in a large corporation. Service is more personal than in large companies (who have to train their people how to be more personable).

Minuses

-    Small businesses do not often pay well, unless they are a boutique consisting of credentialed professionals. Many do not offer benefits, while those that do offer only minimal coverage.

-    There is often more risk associated with a small business. Three out of every four fail.

-    Many small businesses are family-owned, which can create uncomfortable group dynamics for non-family members.

-    You will not get famous working for a small business, for small business leaders are not lionized in the same way that billionaire corporate tycoons are.

-    Regulatory requirements, particularly those having to do with the paperwork that sustains so much government employment, represent a significant burden for everyone in a small business, largely because there is no specialized staff to deal with it.

Start-ups

Somewhere between and beyond corporations and small businesses are the start-ups. These are organizations created from the merger of a promising technology and cash from angel investors or venture capitalists. It is very trendy to work for a start-up because of the well-reported stories about "dot.com millionaires" suffering from "sudden wealth syndrome".

Pluses

+   Lots of excitement, hope, passion, potential.
+   There is a possibility of making it rich on stock options if and when the company goes public.
+   There can be tremendous camaraderie in a company committed to making a dream reality.
+   The start-up environment is much less formal than a corporation. There are few rules, if any. People pretty much dress the way they want.
+   There is a much greater opportunity to make a real and noticeable impact in a start-up because your efforts aren't buried in a bureaucratic structure.
+   Start-ups work at top-speed and there is very little time for boredom.

Minuses

-    There is a 80% chance that the start-up will never go public and that your stock options will be worthless.
-    Start-ups can burn people out very quickly with incredibly long hours and an environment of constant change and high velocity. If you value your social life, stay the hell away from start-ups.
-    Start-ups often lack any sense of order, which can be very disorienting to people who prefer structure.
-    Physical space is usually a problem. Start-ups grow quickly, cram people wherever they might fit and change locations frequently.

- The visionary at the heart of the start-up may be a control freak unwilling to let go of decision-making authority.

Volunteer Work

This is one area where there is no shortage of opportunity. Then again, you do not get paid for your work.

Volunteer work can be an excellent way to explore avenues while meeting your responsibilities to community. Even with the lack of compensation, volunteer work offers rewards. Whether you volunteer for a social cause or an arts group or the local church or the PTA, volunteering can give you the opportunity to learn more about an avenue as well as give you the chance to make a contribution to something you feel is important.

The downsides of volunteering fall into two categories. The first is that some organizations do not know what to do with their volunteers. Potential applications of volunteer talent are wasted when organizations limit volunteers to roles such as "we just need someone to cover the front desk" or "just watch what he's doing and follow along." The other downside to volunteering has to do with certain personality types. Martyrs often attempt to use volunteer work to rescue their sense of self-worth, and while validation of self is a positive goal, seeking it recklessly is both damaging to the person and to the organization.—

Pluses

+ Numerous volunteer opportunities exist in nearly every field of endeavor. Organizations welcome people they do not have to pay and many non-profits can use the help.
+ Volunteering is an opportunity to check out possibilities for income generation before making a full commitment to a particular path.
+ The work itself can be satisfying, as the mission of most non-profits involves responsibility to community.
+ You can meet new people and make new connections without having to engage in the artificiality of networking.

Minuses

-   Volunteering can represent a significant time commitment, depending on the nature of the job.
-   Some organizations manage their volunteers very badly, giving them only menial jobs and failing to apply individual talents to organizational problems.
-   Volunteering is a risky proposition for those who have a natural tendency to work themselves into the ground; martyrs, for instance.
-   There is no pay and too frequently, little recognition.

REFERENCES

Elton, Ben, *Popcorn*. (New York: Pocket Books, 1997), 83.

Fusell, Paul, *Class*. (New York: Touchstone, 1992), 19.

Handy, Charles. *The Age of Unreason*. (Boston: Harvard Business School Press, 1990), 57.

Semler, Ricardo, *Maverick*. (New York: Warner Books, 1993), 166.